In common things that round us lie

Some random truths he can impart,—

The harvest of a quiet eye

That broods and sleeps on his own heart.

Wordsworth

HARVEST OF A QUIET EYE

THE NATURAL WORLD OF JOHN BURROUGHS

Photographs and text selections

—from the writings of John Burroughs—

by Charles F. Davis

With an introduction by Edwin Way Teale

Tamarack Press

Madison, Wisconsin

To Elaine, who made it possible, and to Dalya, whose possibilities await her, this book is lovingly dedicated.

Library of Congress Cataloging in Publication Data
Burroughs, John, 1837-1921.
    Harvest of a quiet eye.

    1. Natural history.   2. Burroughs, John, 1837-1921.
    I. Davis, Charles F., 1927-   II. Title.
QH45.5.B85   500.9'08   76-9
ISBN 0-915024-06-3

Edited by Jill Weber Dean.

Designed by Phill Thill.

Typeset by Fleetwood Graphics.

Printed in the United States of America by Litho Productions, Incorporated.

First printing 1976.

The author is grateful to the following publishers and individuals for permission to reproduce excerpts from copyrighted material.

Elizabeth Burroughs Kelly, for quotations from the journals and letters of John Burroughs.

Harriet Barrus Shatraw, for quotations from *Whitman and Burroughs, Comrades,* Houghton Mifflin, 1931.

Farida A. Wiley, for quotations from *Theodore Roosevelt's America,* Devin-Adair, 1955.

Doubleday & Company, Inc., for quotations from *My Boyhood,* by John Burroughs. Copyright © 1922 by Doubleday & Company, Inc.

Houghton Mifflin Company, for quotations from: *John Burroughs Talks,* by Clifton Johnson, Copyright © 1922 by Houghton Mifflin Company;
The Seer of Slabsides, by Dallas Lore Sharp, Copyright © 1911, 1921 by Dallas Lore Sharp.

The author is indebted to the following individuals and organizations for providing historic photographs.

Elizabeth Burroughs Kelly: 12, 17, 21 lower, 23, 51, 77, 82, 87, 110, 143.

Harriet Barrus Shatraw: 21 upper, 151.

Mr. and Mrs. John Thomson: 146.

The American Museum of Natural History: 55, 140.

CONTENTS

PREFACE

In his profound and sensitive book *In Defense of Nature*, John Hay puts one of the central questions of the day as well as anyone has. "How," he asks, "can a man like myself, soaked with news, his senses muffled, shielded by the mechanics of his civilization and worn into despair by its brutalities, how can he know the real earth when he meets it? How can he be fit company for it?"

This book results from my attempts to meet and know the earth and to become, if I can after so long away, fit company for it. I am fortunate indeed to have found as perceptive, as poetic, and as congenial a guide as John Burroughs. Scaled to more mortal proportions than Thoreau, and, if anything, a more accurate naturalist, the gentle Burroughs makes it all seem within reach of those of us without special gifts or talents for natural history. Refusing to be either scientist or moralist, Burroughs stays with his readers, never leaving them behind in the clouds of specialized erudition beloved of some writers, never demanding of them a purity possible only to the very few. He is, perhaps more than any other, the layman's naturalist.

In making and choosing the photographs for *Harvest of a Quiet Eye*, I was guided by John Burroughs' maxim that the messages of nature lie close at hand. I photographed the world around me rather than making a point (except once) of journeying to "Burroughs country." I did not attempt to illustrate Burroughs' writings. Instead, I tried to make the best pictures I could, trusting that Burroughs' words and my photographs would be sufficiently of one spirit to live amicably within the pages of a single book.

If this book, this combination of images and text that has been so vital a part of the beginnings of my quest for my natural roots, should in any way speak to the yearnings of others and move them to seek out nature for themselves, that would be, for me, a most gratifying outcome.

I gratefully acknowledge the gracious cooperation of the following people: Elizabeth Burroughs Kelly, who supplied historical photographs and reviewed the biography; Miss Farida A. Wiley, of the John Burroughs Memorial Association; Mrs. T. Howard Smith and Mr. Walter Meade, of the Roxbury Burroughs Club; and Harriet Barrus Shatraw, who provided additional historical photographs.

C.F.D.
Oak Park, Illinois
January 1976

INTRODUCTION

Writing of the work of W. H. Hudson, half a century ago, John Galsworthy observed: "Writers are to their readers little new worlds to be explored." The world of John Burroughs, as revealed in his books, as shaped by his individual viewpoint and background, is of special significance in a time like the present. For his is a world of simple, enduring things, a world of closeness to nature, a world of one who, as he said in his most famous poem, "Waiting," walked "amid the eternal ways."

In his first published book, *Notes on Walt Whitman as Poet and Person,* before he had begun writing the nature essays that made him famous, John Burroughs set down his outlook on nature, the point of view that was to run through all his long series of books, in these evocative words: "The birds of the naturalist can never interest us like the thrush the farm boy heard singing in the cedars at twilight as he drove the cows to pasture, or like that swallow that flew gleefully in the air above him as he picked the stones from the early May meadows."

This freshness of the farm boy's outlook is always a characteristic of the best of Burroughs' pages. His books are drawn mainly from his own experiences, his own observations, his own contacts with the land. I once asked a friend who had known Burroughs what the man was like. "He always impressed me," my friend replied, "as a simple, farmerlike man." Burroughs' writings were, in truth, the "harvest of a quiet eye." And it is heartening to see—so many years after they first appeared in print—selections from his numerous volumes gathered together in so beautifully an illustrated and published book as the one you hold in your hand.

On a December night in the year 1893, sitting alone by the fire in his small bark-covered study overlooking the Hudson River, Burroughs read over some of the chapters of his earliest books. "I could have wept over them," he noted in his journal at the time, "they were so fresh and joyous, so untouched by the fret and fever of the world."

Today, even after the passage of so many other nights and days, in a time when the fever of the world has risen so much higher, those who read this compilation from his writings may experience something of the same emotion. A sense of fundamental calm pervades the pages. The fresh dew of morning seems to lie over many of them. They provide a needed antidote for the nervous, tense, hurried and harried life of our late-twentieth-century world.

In a letter to his friend Myron Benton about a rowboat trip he had made down the Delaware River in 1879, Burroughs commented: "I had no adventures, and no hair-breadth escapes; and but little to write about, but you know a writer gets only the seed-corn of his article from without, he grows the main crop himself, as he writes; at least I do." On another occasion, he said: "I've written my books not to please others, but to please myself." And again: "I go to Nature for love of her, and the book follows, or not, as the case may be." In his writing, as his biographer, Clara Barrus, pointed out in her *The Life and Letters of John Burroughs,* he never stuck to a thing just to finish it. When he tired, he got up and turned to something else. It is this leisurely, unforced element in his life that is reflected in his writings.

Those who fell most deeply under his spell were those who knew him in his native surroundings. And no other American author has been more approachable or accessible than John Burroughs. With the exception of George Bernard Shaw, probably no other author of this century was photographed more often. Visitors to Slabsides, the rustic retreat he built in the woods a mile and a half from his home in the village of West Park, New York, ranged from bevies of Vassar students who came regularly from across the Hudson, and distinguished visitors from abroad, to Theodore Roosevelt when he was President of the United States.

In time the interminable interruptions became an increasing burden to him. "What shall I do," he asked, "to check this flood of company?" Describing himself in later life, Burroughs confessed: "I am like an unfenced common—people run over me and through me." But a number of those who made pilgrimages to Slabsides have left charming little glimpses of the naturalist on his home ground. One recalled accompanying him to a spring for a bucket of drinking water. On the way back, while stopping to look at something, Burroughs put the bucket down. A collie came along and drank some of the contents. The companion reported that Burroughs chided the dog a little, "poured a little of the water over the edge, saying, 'I guess the rascal didn't hurt it,' and carried what was left along the path to the cabin."

During the last years of the nineteenth century and the early years of the twentieth century, the more voluble and less perceptive of Burroughs' many followers sought to elevate the importance of his work by downgrading the writings of Henry Thoreau. Burroughs himself had numerous criticisms of Thoreau's natural history. In many of them he was right, but not in all. In the *Century Magazine*, in 1882, he took Thoreau to task for reporting to have heard a whippoorwill in September. One wonders how Burroughs, in all the autumns of his country life, missed hearing the whippoorwill in that brief but well-known period when the bird begins calling again. Thoreau and Burroughs, it is interesting to remember, noted new things in their writings about the same ground-nesting warbler, the ovenbird. Thoreau was the first to give a description of the "rodent

run" by which it draws intruders away from its nest, and Burroughs was the first to put its call into the familiar *Teacher! Teacher! TEACHER!*

It should be pointed out that all during the controversy, Burroughs tried to discourage the comparison between himself and Thoreau. "Why compare *me* to the disadvantage of Thoreau?" he wrote to a friend. "Thoreau is my master in many ways—much nearer the stars than I am—less human, maybe, but more divine—more heroic . . . ." Long since, the misguided comparison with Thoreau, to Thoreau's discredit, has died down. The dweller at Walden Pond and the inhabitant of Slabsides each, in his own way, wrote about nature.

Of the two, Thoreau had the more original mind. He was more gifted in condensing his thoughts and observations into fresh, flavorful, and unforgettable sentences. In his writings the rich grains of thought are scattered everywhere. In Burroughs' pages the grains are further apart. But when they are encountered, they, too, are nourishing and sweet. It is not for penetrating thoughts compressed into memorable epigrams that we go to Burroughs. Nor is it for scientific information that we turn to his books. It is for something else— something deep, something fundamental. It is as though, in his best pages, he has touched a vein of living water, clear and refreshing. We seem, ourselves, to be in contact with the sweetness of the earth—its wholesomeness, its sanity, and its health.

Any writer of the past must be considered in the context of the time in which he lived. In John Burroughs' day, fine-sounding sentences, even though they were divorced from reality—such sentences as "The Lord tempers the wind to the shorn lamb"—were greatly in vogue. Occasionally an echo appears in his writings and correspondence, as in: "I tapped the trees, gathered the sap, and boiled it down in the open air to

10

the calls of bluebirds and robins, and the sugar has a flavor that only bird songs can give it." Charming as is the beginning of the sentence, the ending rings a false note for a modern ear. Again, in Burroughs' time modern fieldguides and powerful binoculars were unknown. Identification was made from birds shot and held in the hand. This must be remembered in recalling the cane-gun Burroughs carried on his early nature walks and his advice to a woman correspondent: "As to shooting the birds, I think a real lover of nature will indulge in no sentimentalism on the subject. Shoot them, of course, and no toying about it." As time passed, however, his outlook gradually altered. Later in life he noted: "A more intimate and harmonious relation is established between me and Nature. I do not outrage the woods; I do not hunt down a bird."

Old places, old friends, old times were always precious to John Burroughs. "Oh, the spell of the Past!" he wrote in his journal on March 22, 1910. "I sit here and look across the river to that palace of the multimillionaire with indifference, or contempt. It means nothing to me; but when in the spring, in my boyhood, I used to look across the home valley and see at night the sugar camp-fire of Seymour Older, in the woods on the side of the big mountain, how much that meant to me!" He declared he was, in his interests, as local as a turtle. "My thoughts go and scratch with the hens, they nip the new grass with the geese, they follow the wild ducks northward."

One hundred five years have now passed since the publication of Burroughs' first nature book, *Wake-Robin*. Fifty-five years have gone by since his death on March 29, 1921, and his burial on April 3, his eighty-fourth birthday, beside Boyhood Rock on the old farm near Roxbury, New York. In these intervening years, how many books have been printed? How many authors have seen their fame increase and fade away?

How many of the great names of the past have become almost forgotten? And yet the quieter fame of John Burroughs has survived. Why has interest in him and his writings endured? Why has it outlived two world wars, those chasms that swallowed so many reputations? What is the secret of the longevity of John Burroughs' appeal?

During his lifetime, of course, his reputation benefited greatly from such things as his highly publicized journey to the Yellowstone with Theodore Roosevelt, his camping trips with Henry Ford and Thomas A. Edison, and the violence of the "nature fakers" controversy that his article "True and Sham Natural History" in *Atlantic Monthly* set off. While he was alive, it was difficult to disentangle the effects of the limelight and the high-pressure publicity from the effects of the works he had produced. It was difficult to assess the real basis for his tremendous popularity.

Both the fact that he became a symbol of a way of life and the fact that his mature appearance was patriarchal—suggesting some white-bearded biblical prophet—played a part. So did the wide use of his essays as collateral reading in schools. And since his death, the continuing activity of the John Burroughs Memorial Association, headquartered in The American Museum of Natural History in New York City, and the publicity surrounding its annual presentation of the Burroughs Medal for distinguished writing in the field of natural history, have kept his life and work before the nation.

But neither controversy nor appearance nor association with famous names nor the efforts of a namesake organization can account entirely for an interest that has survived so long. It is Burroughs' written words and not the trappings of publicity that have kept his name alive. His books have within themselves the seeds of longevity, an appeal that endures. He benefits greatly from selection, as was so clearly demonstrated with the publication of Farida A. Wiley's *John Burroughs' America* in 1951.

In 1895 D. Appleton & Company issued a new edition of Gilbert White's classic *The Natural History of Selborne.* The foreword was written by John Burroughs. Contemplating this same mystery of a writer's lasting influence, he wrote: "So many learned and elaborate treatises have sunk beneath the waves upon which this cockle-shell of a boat rides so safely and buoyantly! What is the secret of its longevity? It is simple and wholesome, like bread or meat or milk. Perhaps it is this same unstrained quality that keeps the book alive." So it is with the books of John Burroughs. They bear out his declaration: "I am bound to praise the simple life because I have lived it and found it good."

It may be that the appeal of his writings is largely lost on those who spend their lives completely in artificial surroundings, who see the morning dew only on brick and asphalt. I suppose, in fact, Burroughs could not be said to be in the main current of life in the present day. But he is somewhere much better to be. He is amid simple, enduring, natural things; things that are part of "eternal ways."

Once more in his bark study overlooking the Hudson, John Burroughs made an entry in his journal, this time on January 9, 1897, at the age of fifty-nine. "Here I sit," he wrote, "night after night, year after year, alone in my little Study perched upon a broad slope of the Hudson, my light visible from afar . . ."

It is reassuring to all of us who cherish nature and nature writing that the light of his books is still seen from afar, that they continue to reappear in new forms for later generations to read.

Edwin Way Teale

John Burroughs, center, was born on April 3, 1837, in an unpainted farmhouse on this 320-acre homestead near the village of Roxbury in New York's Catskill Mountains. He was the seventh of ten children born to Chauncey A. Burroughs and Amy Kelly Burroughs.

NATIVE IN A RARE SENSE

In a one-room schoolhouse near Roxbury in the Catskill Mountains of New York in the 1840s, two schoolboy chums had their desks. Both were to become famous, but in different ways and for vastly different accomplishments. One was Jay Gould, financier, railway tycoon, market manipulator, gold speculator. The other was John Burroughs, vintager, naturalist, essayist, gentle patron of fields and wilds. Today, Gould is memorialized by Tiffany windows in a fine stone chuch; Burroughs, by a simple plaque on a drift boulder in a mountain cow pasture—a rock on which he spent many hours in quiet contemplation of his native hills, and at the foot of which, when death overtook him, he was buried.

About the time of the Revolutionary War, one Ephraim Burroughs moved his large family from Connecticut to Delaware County, New York, and began a homestead. In 1795 one of his sons, Eden Burroughs, cut a road through the woods and over the mountain to another valley, where he established a homestead of his own. In 1826 one of Eden Burroughs' sons, Chauncey Burroughs, settled on a neighboring farm and built the house in which his son John was born in 1837.

I was the son of a farmer, who was the son of a farmer, who was again the son of a farmer. There are no professional or commercial people in my line for several generations, my blood has the flavor of the soil in it; it is rural to the last drop.

Farmers with a decided religious bent contributed the main elements of my personality. I was a countryman died in the wool, yea, more than that, born and bred in the bone, and my character is fundamentally religious . . . . I used to feel that my religious temperament was as clearly traceable to the hard Calvinism of my father as the stratified sandstone to the old granite rock, but that it had undergone a sea change, or in my case, a science change through the activity of the mind and of the age in which I lived. It was rationalism touched with mysticism and warm with the poetic emotion.

The Old School Baptists, of which Chauncey Burroughs was one, felt that religion was too solemn and weighty a matter for children and did not provide religious education for the young. Religion was acquired by Divine, not pedagogical, inspiration. This left son John free to roam the woods and fields on Sundays.

I think this Sunday-school in the woods and fields was, in my case, best. It has always seemed, and still seems, as if I could be a little more intimate with Nature on Sunday than on a week-day; our relations were and are more ideal, a different spirit is abroad, the spirit of holiday and not of work, and I could in youth, and can now, abandon myself to the wild life about me more fully and more joyously on that day than on any other.

John Burroughs was the odd one in his family, the different one, the "one with all the brains," the reflective one, the one who cared deeply about things his brothers and sisters barely noticed. Much of this difference, he thought, came from his mother's people and derived from their Celtic ancestry. He saw something of himself in his grandfather Kelly, soldier of the Revolution, dreamer, raconteur of ghost stories, trout fisherman without peer, and avid reader of the Bible.

He went from the Book to the stream, and from the stream to the Book with great regularity; and when past eighty would woo the trout-streams with all his early fervor. From him I get my dreamy, shirking ways; from him, too, I get that almost feminine sensibility and tinge of melancholy that shows in my books. That emotional Celt, in-effectual in some ways, full of longings and impossible dreams—temporizing, revolutionary, mystical—surely that man is in me, and surely he comes from my Revolutionary ancestor, Gran'ther Kelly.

For a sensitive, intelligent, curious youth, it was not enough to be able to reach out and touch nature in an uninformed, unthinking way. As a child, Burroughs had studied the bumblebees and had given names of his own to the different kinds. But as he grew, the childish concepts and the child-given names were insufficient. Means had to be found to know more thoroughly the facts of nature and to bring that knowledge into relationship with the mind and heart. In this, Emerson played a large part.

I suppose Emerson influenced me most, beginning when I was about nineteen; I had read Pope and Thomson and Young and parts of Shakespeare before that, but they did not kindle this love of nature in me. Emerson did. Though he did not directly treat of outdoor themes, yet his spirit seemed to blend with Nature, and to reveal the ideal and spiritual values in her works. I think it was this, or something like it, that stimulated me and made bird and tree and sky and flower full of a new interest. It is not nature for its own sake that has mainly drawn me; had it been so, I should have turned out a strict man of science; but nature for the soul's sake—the inward world of ideals and emotions. It is this that allies me to the poets; while it is my interest in the mere fact that allies me to the men of science.

The young Burroughs longed to continue his education beyond the local school, but circumstances were strict and finances limited, and he was able to have only six months of formal higher education. A logical vocation for a youthful farm boy who excelled in school was himself to teach in a country school, and John Burroughs be-

came a schoolteacher. While teaching at the Tongore school, near Olive, New York, he met and married Ursula North, the niece of a school trustee. A country teacher's salary was not a living wage for a young man with a wife, so, after a number of unsuccessful attempts at making money, Burroughs packed up and went to Washington, D.C., to seek government employment. It was the Washington of Abraham Lincoln and the Civil War, but Burroughs was drawn particularly by the prospect of meeting Walt Whitman, whose poems he had begun to read and to admire.

Burroughs' poetic dimension received its greatest nourishment from his long and close friendship with Whitman, a comradeship that began in Washington in 1863 and lasted until Whitman's death in 1892. From Whitman the young naturalist got a frame of reference, a much needed overview; for through reading and through looking closely at nature, Burroughs was discovering a world that the stern and narrow outlook of his forebears could not contain.

What a wonderful man is Walt! what a great, yearning love he has! what a hospitable soul, what soft, gentle ways! what a deep, sympathetic voice! How he listens! The most cosmic and synthetical mind I ever knew, he yet has a wonderful power of analysis—keen, searching, discriminating, and subtle.

* * * *

I was trying to express to him how, by some wonderful indirection, I was helped by my knowledge of the birds, the animals, the cows, and common objects. He could see, he said. The ancients had an axiom that he who knew one truth, knew all truths. There are so many ways by which Nature may be come at, so many sides to her, whether by bird, or insect, or flower, or hunting, or science—when one thing is really known, you can no longer be deceived. You possess a key, a standard. You effect an entrance, and everything else links on and follows.

* * * *

He thinks natural history, to be true to life, must be inspired, as well as poetry. There ought to be intuitive perception of truth, important conclusions ought to be jumped to—laws, facts, results arrived at by a kind of insight or inspirational foreknowledge that never could be obtained by mere observation or actual verification. In science—in astronomy—some of the most important discoveries seem inspirations, or a kind of winged, ecstatic reasoning, quite above and beyond the real facts.

The benefits of the friendship did not flow only one way. If Burroughs got from Whitman the grand sweep, the cosmic view, he returned to the poet the specific, particular instances from which the great statements spring.

I related to him our Adirondack trip ... which so pleased him that he said seriously he should make a 'leaf of grass' about it. I related to him other country experiences which he relished hugely. In the spring he wants to go out to my home with me to make sugar, and get a taste of that kind of life.

John Burroughs was one of Whitman's earliest champions. Indeed, his first book, published in 1867, was a defense of Whitman titled *Notes on Walt Whitman as Poet and Person.* And it was in Washington, in company with Whitman and others, that the foundations of Burroughs' work and style were laid. He wrote nature articles for magazines and saw *Wake-Robin,* his first nature book, into print. In 1871 his job with the Treasury Department took him to England, where his friendship with Whitman opened literary doors to him, including the greatest privilege for any young essayist of the day, a visit with Carlyle.

In 1873, after nine years as a clerk in the Treasury Department, the call of rural life over-

powered Burroughs. He resigned his position, bought land along the Hudson River at West Park—midway between the cultural and literary world of New York City and the woods and streams of his native Catskills—and became a farmer again. Work as a bank examiner provided the financial flooring as he built his house and developed his vineyards. This estate, which he called Riverby, was home base for the rest of his life. At Riverby he grew choice table grapes and wrote the essays and books that made him America's best-loved nature writer for fifty years. At Riverby he raised his son, Julian, and saw his grandchildren born. From Riverby he set off on travels to Europe, Jamaica, Alaska, Hawaii, and many parts of the United States. At Riverby, too, and at a number of rustic retreats he built later, he was host to the many people, famous and obscure, who were drawn by his writings to seek him out.

The Riverby years were not eventful in the grand sense, but of those half-hidden happenings that are the true history of the earth—and the true stuff of nature writing—there were plenty: spring flowers, birds' nests, autumn leaves, "days of great freshness and beauty."

... Julian and I go to the woods; no flowers yet; ants just out languidly patrolling their mounds. Frog-spawn in the pools. We sit a long time on a rock in the woods and enjoy the genial warmth and the clean open woods, with the creek glancing and murmuring below us.

* * * *

Yesterday and today are the shining days. How the river dances and sparkles, how the new leaves of all the trees shine under the sun! The air has a soft lustre; there is a haze; it is not blue, but a kind of shining, diffused nimbus—no clouds, but the sky is a bluish-white, very soft and delicate.

* * * *

Paused a while this morning, in returning from the post office, to see the stems of the leaves of the ash fall. The leaves were off some days ago, and this morning the stems were falling in the still air, coming down swiftly, one by one.

If the world beat a path to John Burroughs' doorstep, it was because the world was at his doorstep already; his were but the eyes to see it and the pen to tell of it. And the spirit to relate it all to the human heart.

As the Washington years were a period of literary apprenticeship, so life at Riverby was a time of centering down and maturing as an observer of nature and writer upon its themes. Open to nature by temperament, Burroughs was able to translate a wordless closeness with nature into words of rare power and charm.

But this weakness of the I in me is probably a great help to me as a writer upon Nature. I do not stand in my own light. I am pure spirit, pure feeling, and get very close to bird and beast. My thin skin lets the shy and delicate influences pass. I can surrender myself to Nature without effort. I am like her. That which hinders me with men, and makes me weak and ill at ease in their presence, makes me strong with impersonal Nature, and admits me to her influences.

* * * *

One important thing in writing is to divest yourself of any false or accidental mood, or view, or feeling, and get down to your real self, and speak as directly and sincerely as you do about your daily business and affairs ... Get down to your real self—your better real self, and let that speak.

* * * *

Read some chapters in one or two of my books, sitting here alone by the fire, the other night. I could have wept over them—they were so fresh and joyous, so untouched by the fret and fever of the world. Where was the paradise I lived in when I wrote those books? Here, right here, where I now live. A kind of perennial youth breathes in those books. No merit of mine. I could not help it.

In 1895, at the age of fifty-seven, Burroughs wrote in his journal, *New book [Riverby] came to-day. Doubtless the last of my outdoor series. I look it over with a sigh. For a quarter of a century I have been writing these books—living them first, and then writing them out. What serene joy I have had in gathering this honey! and now I begin to feel that it is about over with me—my interest, my curiosity, are getting blunted.*

In truth, he was entering the most productive period of his life. Over the next twenty-six years, sixteen more books emerged from his several rustic studies. He was, to be sure, moving away from the literary recording of the natural world. His succeeding works became more and more philosophical, though rooted always in nature. He enjoyed the friendship of some of the best-known people of the day, and was a considerable celebrity in his own right.

In 1881 he had built a one-room study —the Bark Study—below the main house at Riverby, where he could read and work undisturbed. By 1895 he felt the need for something a little more remote. He acquired some land among the hills about a mile above Riverby and constructed a cabin. He called it Slabsides for the plain reason that the exterior siding was made of slabs. It was to Slabsides, conceived as a retreat from visitors, that visitors flocked, singly and in groups. One of the earliest of these was John Muir—John o'Mountains come to call on John o'Birds.

John Muir came last night. Julian and I met him at Hyde Park. A very interesting man; a little prolix at times. You must not be in a hurry, or have any pressing duty, when you start his stream of talk and adventure .... He is a poet, and almost a seer; something ancient and far-away in the look

John Burroughs in 1857, from an etching owned by the American Academy of Arts and Letters. From 1854 to 1863, Burroughs spent much of his time teaching at country schools, mainly in New York and New Jersey, but also in Buffalo Grove, Illinois.

Burroughs seated at his boyhood desk in the West Settlement school. The only member of his family with intellectual aspirations, he was, nonetheless, an indifferent student, making frequent requests to go outside and wash his slate, and avoiding compositions whenever possible.

of his eyes . . . . he must have a continent for his playground. He starts off for a walk, after graduation, and walks from Wisconsin to Florida . . . Probably the truest lover of Nature, as she appears in woods, mountains, glaciers, we have yet had.

In 1899 Burroughs was invited to participate in an expedition to Alaska sponsored by E. H. Harriman. He was to be the historian for the expedition, which was made up of some forty scientists, artists, and other experts, including John Muir. Burroughs' impressions formed part of the official record of the expedition, but he was not pleased with the narrative.

A thing has to stay in my consciousness for a while and develop there before I can reproduce it satisfactorily. If I could have waited six months or more—until I felt moved to write, I might have brought forth something more creditable. But they made me go about it deliberately, before I had carried it long enough. That is not my way of writing—I go to Nature for love of her, and the book follows, or not, as the case may be.

Burroughs first met Theodore Roosevelt in Washington in 1889, when the latter was a member of the Civil Service Commission. In 1903, when Roosevelt was President, he invited Burroughs to accompany him on a camping trip to Yellowstone Park. Although it was to be a vacation from the duties of the presidency for Roosevelt, the trip west on the presidential train had many of the trappings of a campaign: official receptions, dinners, and whistle-stop speeches. At nearly every stop, readers of Burroughs' books approached the train; some, to the delight of Roosevelt, had come to see the author, not the President.

Later the same year, the President and Mrs. Roosevelt were guests at Slabsides. Between Theodore Roosevelt—soldier, adventurer, big-game hunter, tireless public figure—and John Burroughs—gentle wooer of nature's smaller

secrets, celebrity in spite of himself—there existed a great bond of friendship and mutual respect. Each had qualities the other admired, and both were keen observers of nature.

He [Roosevelt] was a naturalist on the broadest grounds, uniting much technical knowledge of the daily lives and habits of all forms of wildlife. He probably knew tenfold more natural history than all the presidents who preceded him, and, I think one is safe in saying, more human history also.

As a young man, Burroughs had been an avid hunter of birds, shooting and mounting many in connection with his ornithological studies, and he was a keen fisherman all his life. But as he grew older, the killing of wildlife became more and more distasteful to him, and he could wield a scathing pen at hunters when their practices offended him. Roosevelt, however, not only escaped his wrath, but had his approval.

I have never been disturbed by the President's hunting trips. It is to such men as he that the big game legitimately belongs,—men who regard it from the point of view of the naturalist as well as from that of the sportsman, who are interested in its preservation, and who share with the world the delight they experience in the chase. Such a hunter as Roosevelt is as far removed from the game-butcher as day is from night; and as for his killing of the "varmints,"—bears, cougars and bobcats,—the fewer of these there are, the better for the useful and beautiful game.

Astute as he was in foreseeing the depredations of an industrialized society upon the natural world, Burroughs seems not to have anticipated the view, now gaining favor, that predators have a positive and proper role to play in the natural scheme of things. Indeed, his writings are not rich in suggestions of ecology as that word is now understood. It was a concept whose hour had not yet come round.

Much as he loved his sojourns in the wilderness, much as untamed places appealed to him, Burroughs was first and always a countryman, a pastoralist. If he thrilled to the primal landscapes of Alaska, sought the mountain fastnesses of the Adirondacks, or tramped the remoter regions of the Catskills, it was from the pasture he went, it was to the tilled field and snug barn he returned. Even Slabsides was located in wilderness modified, wilderness on the rim. At its core there was tilled land, a celery bog drained from the original swamp.

In fact it has been the land that has given me most pleasure in my wilderness home. It looks different from other land. It is land I have made and is much more precious than any I could buy. Before I took hold of it there was nothing in this hollow of the woods except a bit of untamed nature, and my land was buried beneath trees, stumps, and bog. I had to fight for it, and land you get that way you value. Yes, it is wonderful land—land I've created myself. If some one had given me a nice piece of tillable land, I wouldn't have thought anything of it compared with my swamp.

Although John Burroughs was the odd one of the family, the different one, he was never a stranger among his people. It is unlikely that his father or brothers ever read a word he wrote. Though they could not share John's world, he could, and did, share theirs. He loved his family intensely. His relatives and his native hills were central to him all his life, and he made it a point to visit both each year.

My native mountain, out of whose loins I sprang, is called the Old Clump. It sits there, looking southward and holding the home farm in its lap . . . . Old Clump figured a good deal in my boyhood life and scarcely less in my life since. The first deer's horn I ever saw we found there one Sunday morning under a jutting rock as we were on our way to the summit. My excursions to salt and count the sheep often took me there, and my boyhood thirst for the wild and adventurous took me there still oftener. Old Clump used to lift me up into the air three thousand feet and introduce me to his great brotherhood of mountains far and near and make me acquainted with the exhilaration that awaits one on mountain tops.

With advancing years, the urge to return to his birthplace became increasingly strong. In the fall of 1910 he began repairs on a farmhouse that had belonged to his brother Curtis. The house was situated on the east end of the Burroughs family homestead. He called it Woodchuck Lodge in honor of the original titleholders, whose descendants continued to thrive in the surrounding fields. Here he spent his remaining summers.

Those hills comfort me as no other place in the world does. Why should I not spend more of my time there? . . . It is home there,—the only real home I ever had. Elsewhere I have been merely a camper for a night . . . . They are a part of my being. You see I am a real autochthon. These hills fathered and mothered me. I am blood of their blood and bone of their bone, and why should I not go back to them in my last years?

Burroughs did not simply retire to Woodchuck Lodge and live as the dean emeritus of American nature writers. His last decade was an active, productive, and, for the most part, pleasant one. Between the age of seventy-four and his death ten years later, he wrote eight more books. He received many visitors, answered many letters, and enjoyed a spirited friendship with Henry Ford and Thomas Edison, complete with camping trips to the mountains and driving lessons in the car Ford gave him. The deaths of many of his friends saddened him, and the death of his wife in 1917, though expected, weighed heavily upon him. He was greatly distressed by the World War, threatening as it did to loose upon the world a brutal and barbaric militarism. The Allied victory, he felt, made the world safe for the gentler pursuits he cherished so much.

In response to a request from Dr. Clara Barrus, his biographer, Burroughs undertook, in a series of conversations and letters, to supply some autobiographical observations. In his development as a naturalist and a writer, he laid stress on three factors: his country birth and upbringing, his nonaggressive nature, and the touch of the idler and dreamer that was in him.

When I began, in my twenty-fifth or twenty-sixth year, to write about the birds, I found that I had only to unpack the memories of the farm boy within me to get at the main things about the common ones. I had unconsciously absorbed the knowledge that gave the life and warmth to my page. Take that farm boy out of my books, out of all the pages in which he is latent as well as visibly active, and you have robbed them of something vital and fundamental, you have taken from the soil much of its fertility.

* * * *

I see that my life has been more of a holiday than most persons', much more than was my father's or his father's. I have picnicked all along the way . . . . I have done, for the most part, what I wanted to do. Some drudgery I have had, that is, in uncongenial work on the farm, in teaching, in clerking, in bank-examining; but amid all these things I have kept an outlook, an open door, as it were, out into the free fields of nature, and a buoyant feeling that I would soon be there.

* * * *

I have loved nature, I have loved the animals, I have loved my fellow-men. I have made my own whatever was fair and of good report. I have loved the thoughts of the great thinkers and the poems of the great poets, and the devout lines of the great religious souls. I have not looked afar off for my joy and entertainment, but in things near at hand, that all may have on equal terms

. . . . I have got much satisfaction out of life; it has been worth while.

I have not been a burden-bearer; for shame be it said, perhaps, when there are so many burdens to be borne by some one. I have borne those that came in my way, or that circumstances put upon me, and have at least pulled my own weight. I have had my share of the holiday spirit; I have had a social holiday, a moral holiday, a business holiday. I have gone a-fishing while others were struggling and groaning and losing their souls in the great social or political or business maelstrom. I know, too, I have gone a-fishing while others have labored in the slums and given their lives to the betterment of their fellows. But I have been a good fisherman, and I should have made a poor missionary, or reformer, or leader of any crusade against sin and crime.

* * * *

I shall shock you by telling you I am not much of a patriot. I have but little national pride. If we went to war with a foreign power to-morrow, my sympathies would be with the foreigner if I thought him in the right . . . . I have absolutely no state pride, any more than I have county or town pride, or neighborhood pride. But I make it up in family or tribal affection.

* * * *

I love life, as such, and I am quickly conscious of anything that threatens to check its even flow. I want a full measure of it, and I want it as I do my spring water, clear and sweet and from the original sources. Hence I have always chafed in cities, I must live in the country. Life in the cities is like the water there—a long way from the original sources, and more or less tainted by artificial conditions.

* * * *

The least cloud or film in my mental skies mars or stops my work. I write with my body quite as much as with my mind. How persons

In the autumn of 1857, at age twenty, Burroughs took a weekend's respite from schoolteaching to marry Ursula North. The marriage was not ideal, but after her death—on March 6, 1917—Burroughs wrote, "Felt her loss afresh when I went over to the kitchen door and found the leaves clustered there as if waiting for something. They were waiting for her broom. For over forty years it had not failed them . . . I never could have believed I should miss her so much."

In 1873 Burroughs bought nine acres of land along the Hudson River, near West Park, New York. He named the estate, which eventually totaled twenty acres, Riverby. Here, he built a fine stone house and planted vineyards. Here, too, in 1878 his only child, Julian, was born. Though Burroughs lived at Riverby for nearly fifty years, he always called his parents' farmstead "home."

whose bread of life is heavy, so to speak,—no lightness or buoyancy or airiness at all,—can make good literature is a mystery to me; or those who stimulate themselves with drugs or alcohol or coffee. I would live so that I could get tipsy on a glass of water, or find a spur in a whiff of morning air.

* * *

Life has been to me simply an opportunity to learn and enjoy, and, through my books, to share my enjoyment with others. I have had no other ambition. I have thirsted to know things, and to make the most of them. The universe is to me a grand spectacle that fills me with awe and wonder and joy, and with intense curiosity.

John Burroughs was an immensely popular writer in his day, but his fame did not long survive him. Older people remember him still, but to the rest he is largely unknown. Perhaps the Jazz Age, the Depression, and the Second World War were simply too much competition, and his voice got drowned out by the roar of the twenties and following decades. A gentler, less assertive chronicler than Thoreau or Muir, he is slower than they to come again into his own.

Aside from being the first to publish a description of the nest of the black-throated blue warbler, he broke little new ground, discovered few new things, added few new facts to the sum of knowledge. But to the old, the common, the well-known, he brought new familiarity, new insight, new lustre.

". . . he made discoveries, volumes of them," wrote Dallas Lore Sharp, "contributions largely to our stock of literature, and to our store of love for the earth, and to our joy in living upon it. He turned a little of the universe into literature; translated a portion of the earth into human language; restored to us our garden here eastward in Eden—apple-tree and all."

To do this took quiet, serenity, repose. It took *connection,* not joining or proximity merely, but a state of oneness, kinship, filiation. Of him Walt Whitman said, "He is so calm, so poised, so much at home with himself, so much a familiar spirit of the forests . . . . He is a child of the woods, fields, hills—native to them in a rare sense (in a sense almost of miracle)."

On the twenty-ninth of March, 1921, on a train bearing him back from California, where he had gone for the winter months, John Burroughs died. On April third, his eighty-fourth birthday, he was buried at the foot of his favorite rock in a mountain pasture on the family farm—less than a half mile from the house in which he was born. His last words had been, "How far are we from home?"

As he grew older, Burroughs' longing for his native hills grew stronger. In the autumn of 1910 he began remodeling an old farmhouse on the Burroughs family's homestead near Roxbury, New York. Thereafter, Woodchuck Lodge, as he called it, was his summer home.

All life asks is opportunity; it takes its chances in the clash of opposing forces; it loses at one point and gains at another; the hazards of time and change modify it, hindering it or helping it, but do not extinguish it.

Under the Apple-Trees

For so gentle and on the whole so beneficent an element, the snow asserts itself very proudly. It takes the world quickly and entirely to itself. It makes no concessions or compromises, but rules despotically. It baffles and bewilders the eye, and it returns the sun glare for glare. Its coming in our winter climate is the hand of mercy to the earth and to everything in its bosom, but it is a barrier and an embargo to everything that moves above.

Pepacton

In what bold relief stand out the lives of all walkers of the snow! The snow is a great tell-tale, and blabs as effectually as it obliterates. I go into the woods, and know all that has happened. I cross the fields, and if only a mouse has visited his neighbor, the fact is chronicled.

Winter Sunshine

This was a typical March day, clear, dry, hard, and windy, the river rumpled and crumpled, the sky intense, distant objects strangely near; a day full of strong light, unusual; an extraordinary lightness and clearness all around the horizon, as if there were a diurnal aurora streaming up and burning through the sunlight; smoke from the first spring fires rising up in various directions; a day that winnowed the air, and left no film in the sky.

Signs and Seasons

One seems to get nearer to nature in the early spring days: all screens are removed, the earth everywhere speaks directly to you; she is not hidden by verdure and foliage; there is a peculiar delight in walking over the brown turf of the fields that one cannot feel later on. How welcome the smell of it, warmed by the sun; the first breath of the reviving earth . . . .

Nature is always new in the spring, and lucky are we if it finds us new also.

Riverby

March water is usually clean, sweet water; every brook is a trout brook, a mountain brook; the cold and the snow have supplied the condition of a high latitude; no stagnation, no corruption, comes downstream now as on a summer freshet. Winter comes down, liquid and repentant. Indeed, it is more than water that runs then: it is frost subdued; it is spring triumphant.

Signs and Seasons

Whatever is upon the earth is of the earth; it came out of the divine soil, beamed upon by the fructifying heavens, the soul of man not less than his body.

I never see the spring flowers rising from the mould, or the pond-lilies born of the black ooze, that matter does not become transparent and reveal to me the working of the same celestial powers that fashioned the first man from the common dust.

Man's mind is no more a stranger to the earth than is his body. Is not the clod wise? Is not the chemistry underfoot intelligent? Do not the roots of the trees find their way? Do not the birds know their times and seasons? Are not all things about us filled to overflowing with mind-stuff? The cosmic mind is the earth mind, and the earth mind is man's mind, freed but narrowed, with vision but with erring reason, conscious but troubled, and—shall we say?—human but immortal.

Leaf and Tendril

THE SNOW-WALKERS

He who marvels at the beauty of the world in summer will find equal cause for wonder and admiration in winter. It is true the pomp and the pageantry are swept away, but the essential elements remain,—the day and the night, the mountain and the valley, the elemental play and succession and the perpetual presence of the infinite sky. In winter the stars seem to have rekindled their fires, the moon achieves a fuller triumph, and the heavens wear a look of a more exalted simplicity. Summer is more wooing and seductive, more versatile and human, appeals to the affections and the sentiments, and fosters inquiry and the art impulse. Winter is of a more heroic cast, and addresses the intellect. The severe studies and disciplines come easier in winter. One imposes larger tasks upon himself, and is less tolerant of his own weaknesses.

The tendinous part of the mind, so to speak, is more developed in winter; the fleshy, in summer. I should say winter had given the bone and sinew to Literature, summer the tissues and blood.

The simplicity of winter has a deep moral. The return of nature, after such a career of splendor and prodigality, to habits so simple and austere, is not lost upon either the head or the heart. It is the philosopher coming back from the banquet and the wine to a cup of water and a crust of bread.

And then this beautiful masquerade of the elements,—the novel disguises our nearest friends put on! Here is another rain and another dew, water that will not flow, nor spill, nor receive the taint of an unclean vessel. And if we see truly, the same old beneficence and willingness to serve lurk beneath all.

Look up at the miracle of the falling snow,—the air a dizzy maze of whirling, eddying flakes, noiselessly transforming the world, the exquisite crystals dropping in ditch and gutter, and disguising in the same suit of spotless livery all objects upon which they fall. How novel and fine the first drifts! The old, dilapidated fence is suddenly set off with the most fantastic ruffles, scalloped and fluted after an unheard-of fashion! Looking down a long line of decrepit stone wall, in the trimming of which the wind had fairly run riot, I saw, as for the first time, what a severe yet master artist old Winter is. Ah, a severe artist! How stern the woods look, dark and cold and as rigid against the horizon as iron!

All life and action upon the snow have an added emphasis and significance. Every expression is underscored. Summer has few finer pictures than this winter one of the farmer foddering his cattle from a stack upon the clean snow,—the movement, the sharply defined figures, the great green flakes of hay, the long file of patient cows, the advance just arriving and pressing eagerly for the choicest morsels,—and the bounty and providence it suggests. Or the chopper in the woods,—the prostrate tree, the white new chips scattered about, his easy triumph over the cold, his coat hanging to a limb, and the clear, sharp ring of his axe. The woods are rigid and tense, keyed up by the frost, and resound like a stringed instrument. Or the road-breakers, sallying forth with oxen and sleds in the still, white world, the day after the storm, to restore the lost track and demolish the beleaguering drifts.

All sounds are sharper in winter; the air transmits better. At night I hear more distinctly the steady roar of the North Mountain. In summer it is a sort of complacent purr, as the breezes stroke down its sides; but in winter always the same low, sullen growl.

A severe artist! No longer the canvas and the pigments, but the marble and the chisel. When the nights are calm and the moon full, I go

41

out to gaze upon the wonderful purity of the moonlight and the snow. The air is full of latent fire, and the cold warms me—after a different fashion from that of the kitchen stove. The world lies about me in a "trance of snow." The clouds are pearly and iridescent, and seem the farthest possible remove from the condition of a storm,— the ghosts of clouds, the indwelling beauty freed from all dross. I see the hills, bulging with great drifts, lift themselves up cold and white against the sky, the black lines of fences here and there obliterated by the depth of the snow. Presently a fox barks away up next the mountain, and I imagine I can almost see him sitting there, in his furs, upon the illuminated surface, and looking down in my direction. As I listen, one answers him from behind the woods in the valley. What a wild winter sound, wild and weird, up among the ghostly hills! Since the wolf has ceased to howl upon these mountains, and the panther to scream, there is nothing to be compared with it. So wild! I get up in the middle of the night to hear it. It is refreshing to the ear, and one delights to know that such wild creatures are among us. At this season Nature makes the most of every throb of life that can withstand her severity. How heartily she indorses this fox! In what bold relief stand out the lives of all walkers of the snow! The snow is a great tell-tale, and blabs as effectually as it obliterates. I go into the woods, and know all that has happened. I cross the fields, and if only a mouse has visited his neighbor, the fact is chronicled.

The red fox is the only species that abounds in my locality; the little gray fox seems to prefer a more rocky and precipitous country, and a less rigorous climate; the cross fox is occasionally seen, and there are traditions of the silver gray among the oldest hunters. But the red fox is the sportsman's prize, and the only fur-bearer worthy of note in these mountains. I go out in the morning, after a fresh fall of snow, and see at all points

where he has crossed the road. Here he has leisurely passed within rifle-range of the house, evidently reconnoitring the premises with an eye to the hen-roost. That clear, sharp track,—there is no mistaking it for the clumsy footprint of a little dog. All his wildness and agility are photographed in it. Here he has taken fright, or suddenly recollected an engagement, and in long, graceful leaps, barely touching the fence, has gone careering up the hill as fleet as the wind.

The wild, buoyant creature, how beautiful he is! I had often seen his dead carcass, and at a distance had witnessed the hounds drive him across the upper fields; but the thrill and excitement of meeting him in his wild freedom in the woods were unknown to me till, one cold winter day, drawn thither by the baying of a hound, I stood near the summit of the mountain, waiting a renewal of the sound, that I might determine the course of the dog and choose my position,—stimulated by the ambition of all young Nimrods to bag some notable game. Long I waited, and patiently, till, chilled and benumbed, I was about to turn back, when, hearing a slight noise, I looked up and beheld a most superb fox, loping along with inimitable grace and ease, evidently disturbed, but not pursued by the hound, and so absorbed in his private meditations that he failed to see me, though I stood transfixed with amazement and admiration, not ten yards distant. I took his measure at a glance,—a large male, with dark legs, and massive tail tipped with white,—a most magnificent creature; but so astonished and fascinated was I by this sudden appearance and matchless beauty, that not till I had caught the last glimpse of him, as he disappeared over a knoll, did I awake to my duty as a sportsman, and realize what an opportunity to distinguish myself I had unconsciously let slip. I clutched my gun, half angrily, as if it was to blame, and went home out of humor with myself and all fox-kind. But I have since thought better of the experience, and concluded that I bagged the game after all, the best part of it, and fleeced Reynard of something more valuable than his fur, without his knowledge.

This is thoroughly a winter sound,—this voice of the hound upon the mountain,—and one that is music to many ears. The long trumpet-like bay, heard for a mile or more,—now faintly back in the deep recesses of the mountain,—now distinct, but still faint, as the hound comes over some prominent point and the wind favors,—anon entirely lost in the gully,—then breaking out again much nearer, and growing more and more pronounced as the dog approaches, till, when he comes around the brow of the mountain, directly above you, the barking is loud and sharp. On he goes along the northern spur, his voice rising and sinking as the wind and the lay of the ground modify it, till lost to hearing.

The fox usually keeps half a mile ahead, regulating his speed by that of the hound, occasionally pausing a moment to divert himself with a mouse, or to contemplate the landscape, or to listen for his pursuer. If the hound press him too closely, he leads off from mountain to mountain, and so generally escapes the hunter; but if the pursuit be slow, he plays about some ridge or peak, and falls a prey, though not an easy one, to the experienced sportsman.

A most spirited and exciting chase occurs when the farm-dog gets close upon one in the open field, as sometimes happens in the early morning. The fox relies so confidently upon his superior speed, that I imagine he half tempts the dog to the race. But if the dog be a smart one, and their course lie downhill, over smooth ground, Reynard must put his best foot forward, and then sometimes suffer the ignominy of being run over by his pursuer, who, however, is quite unable to pick him up, owing to the speed. But when they mount the hill, or enter the woods, the superior

nimbleness and agility of the fox tell at once, and he easily leaves the dog far in his rear. For a cur less than his own size he manifests little fear, especially if the two meet alone, remote from the house. In such cases, I have seen first one turn tail, then the other.

A novel spectacle often occurs in summer, when the female has young. You are rambling on the mountain, accompanied by your dog, when you are startled by that wild, half-threatening squall, and in a moment perceive your dog, with inverted tail, and shame and confusion in his looks, sneaking toward you, the old fox but a few rods in his rear. You speak to him sharply, when he bristles up, turns about, and, barking, starts off vigorously, as if to wipe out the dishonor; but in a moment comes sneaking back more abashed than ever, and owns himself unworthy to be called a dog. The fox fairly shames him out of the woods. The secret of the matter is her sex, though her conduct, for the honor of the fox be it said, seems to be prompted only by solicitude for the safety of her young.

One of the most notable features of the fox is his large and massive tail. Seen running on the snow at a distance, his tail is quite as conspicuous as his body; and, so far from appearing a burden, seems to contribute to his lightness and buoyancy. It softens the outline of his movements, and repeats or continues to the eye the ease and poise of his carriage. But, pursued by the hound on a wet, thawy day, it often becomes so heavy and bedraggled as to prove a serious inconvenience, and compels him to take refuge in his den. He is very loath to do this; both his pride and the traditions of his race stimulate him to run it out, and win by fair superiority of wind and speed; and only a wound or a heavy and moppish tail will drive him to avoid the issue in this manner.

To learn his surpassing shrewdness and cunning, attempt to take him with a trap.

Rogue that he is, he always suspects some trick, and one must be more of a fox than he is himself to overreach him. At first sight it would appear easy enough. With apparent indifference he crosses your path, or walks in your footsteps in the field, or travels along the beaten highway, or lingers in the vicinity of stacks and remote barns. Carry the carcass of a pig, or a fowl, or a dog, to a distant field in midwinter, and in a few nights his tracks cover the snow about it.

The inexperienced country youth, misled by this seeming carelessness of Reynard, suddenly conceives a project to enrich himself with fur, and wonders that the idea has not occurred to him before, and to others. I knew a youthful yeoman of this kind, who imagined he had found a mine of wealth on discovering on a remote side-hill, between two woods, a dead porker, upon which it appeared all the foxes of the neighborhood had nightly banqueted. The clouds were burdened with snow; and as the first flakes commenced to eddy down, he set out, trap and broom in hand, already counting over in imagination the silver quarters he would receive for his first fox-skin. With the utmost care, and with a palpitating heart, he removed enough of the trodden snow to allow the trap to sink below the surface. Then, carefully sifting the light element over it and sweeping his tracks full, he quickly withdrew, laughing exultingly over the little surprise he had prepared for the cunning rogue. The elements conspired to aid him, and the falling snow rapidly obliterated all vestiges of his work. The next morning at dawn he was on his way to bring in his fur. The snow had done its work effectually, and, he believed, had kept his secret well. Arrived in sight of the locality, he strained his vision to make out his prize lodged against the fence at the foot of the hill. Approaching nearer, the surface was unbroken, and doubt usurped the place of certainty in his mind. A slight mound marked the site of the porker, but there was no footprint near it. Looking up the hill, he saw where Reynard had walked leisurely down toward his wonted bacon till within a few yards of it, when he had wheeled, and with prodigious strides disappeared in the woods. The young trapper saw at a glance what a comment this was upon his skill in the art, and, indignantly exhuming the iron, he walked home with it, the stream of silver quarters suddenly setting in another direction.

The successful trapper commences in the fall, or before the first deep snow. In a field not too remote, with an old axe he cuts a small place, say ten inches by fourteen, in the frozen ground, and removes the earth to the depth of three or four inches, then fills the cavity with dry ashes, in which are placed bits of roasted cheese. Reynard is very suspicious at first, and gives the place a wide berth. It looks like design, and he will see how the thing behaves before he approaches too near. But the cheese is savory and the cold severe. He ventures a little closer every night, until he can reach and pick a piece from the surface. Emboldened by success, like other mortals, he presently digs freely among the ashes, and, finding a fresh supply of the delectable morsels every night, is soon thrown off his guard and his suspicions quite lulled. After a week of baiting in this manner, and on the eve of a light fall of snow, the trapper carefully conceals his trap in the bed, first smoking it thoroughly with hemlock boughs to kill or neutralize the smell of the iron. If the weather favors and the proper precautions have been taken, he may succeed, though the chances are still greatly against him.

Reynard is usually caught very lightly, seldom more than the ends of his toes being between the jaws. He sometimes works so cautiously as to spring the trap without injury even to his toes, or may remove the cheese night after night without even springing it. I knew an old trapper who, on finding himself outwitted in this manner, tied a bit of cheese to the pan, and next morning had poor Reynard by the jaw. The trap is not fastened, but only encumbered with a clog, and is all the more sure in its hold by yielding to every effort of the animal to extricate himself.

When Reynard sees his captor approaching, he would fain drop into a mouse-hole to render himself invisible. He crouches to the ground and remains perfectly motionless until he perceives himself discovered, when he makes one desperate and final effort to escape, but ceases all struggling as you come up, and behaves in a manner that stamps him a very timid warrior,—cowering to the earth with a mingled look of shame, guilt, and abject fear. A young farmer told me of tracing one with his trap to the border of a wood, where he discovered the cunning rogue trying to hide by embracing a small tree. Most animals, when taken in a trap, show fight; but Reynard has more faith in the nimbleness of his feet than in the terror of his teeth.

Entering the woods, the number and variety of the tracks contrast strongly with the rigid, frozen aspect of things. Warm jets of life still shoot and play amid this snowy desolation. Fox-tracks are far less numerous than in the fields; but those of hares, skunks, partridges, squirrels, and mice abound. The mice tracks are very pretty, and look like a sort of fantastic stitching on the coverlid of the snow. One is curious to know what brings these tiny creatures from their retreats; they do not seem to be in quest of food, but rather to be traveling about for pleasure or sociability, though always going post-haste, and linking stump with stump and tree with tree by fine, hurried strides. That is when they travel openly; but they have hidden passages and winding galleries under the snow, which undoubtedly are their main avenues of communication. Here and there these passages rise so near the surface as to be covered by only a

frail arch of snow, and a slight ridge betrays their course to the eye. I know him well. He is known to the farmer as the "deer mouse," to the naturalist as the white-footed mouse,—a very beautiful creature, nocturnal in his habits, with large ears, and large, fine eyes full of a wild, harmless look. He is daintily marked, with white feet and a white belly. When disturbed by day he is very easily captured, having none of the cunning or viciousness of the common Old World mouse.

It is he who, high in the hollow trunk of some tree, lays by a store of beechnuts for winter use. Every nut is carefully shelled, and the cavity that serves as storehouse lined with grass and leaves. The wood-chopper frequently squanders this precious store. I have seen half a peck taken from one tree, as clean and white as if put up by the most delicate hands,—as they were. How long it must have taken the little creature to collect this quantity, to hull them one by one, and convey them up to his fifth-story chamber! He is not confined to the woods, but is quite as common in the fields, particularly in the fall, amid the corn and potatoes. When routed by the plow, I have seen the old one take flight with half a dozen young hanging to her teats, and with such reckless speed that some of the young would lose their hold and fly off amid the weeds. Taking refuge in a stump with the rest of her family, the anxious mother would presently come back and hunt up the missing ones.

The snow-walkers are mostly night-walkers also, and the record they leave upon the snow is the main clew one has to their life and doings. The hare is nocturnal in its habits, and though a very lively creature at night, with regular courses and run-ways through the wood, is entirely quiet by day. Timid as he is, he makes little effort to conceal himself, usually squatting beside a log, stump, or tree, and seeming to avoid rocks and ledges, where he might be partially housed from the cold and the snow, but where also—and this consideration undoubtedly determines his choice—he would be more apt to fall a prey to his enemies. In this, as well as in many other respects, he differs from the rabbit proper: he never burrows in the ground, or takes refuge in a den or hole, when pursued. If caught in the open fields, he is much confused and easily overtaken by the dog; but in the woods, he leaves him at a bound. In summer, when first disturbed, he beats the ground violently with his feet, by which means he would express to you his surprise or displeasure; it is a dumb way he has of scolding. After leaping a few yards, he pauses an instant, as if to determine the degree of danger, and then hurries away with a much lighter tread.

His feet are like great pads, and his track has little of the sharp, articulated expression of Reynard's, or of animals that climb or dig. Yet it is very pretty like all the rest, and tells its own tale. There is nothing bold or vicious or vulpine in it, and his timid, harmless character is published at every leap. He abounds in dense woods, preferring localities filled with a small undergrowth of beech and birch, upon the bark of which he feeds. Nature is rather partial to him, and matches his extreme local habits and character with a suit that corresponds with his surroundings,—reddish gray in summer and white in winter.

The sharp-rayed track of the partridge adds another figure to this fantastic embroidery upon the winter snow. Her course is a clear, strong line, sometimes quite wayward, but generally very direct, steering for the densest, most impenetrable places,—leading you over logs and through brush, alert and expectant, till, suddenly, she bursts up a few yards from you, and goes humming through the trees,—the complete triumph of endurance and vigor. Hardy native bird, may your tracks never be fewer, or your visits to the birch-tree less frequent!

The squirrel tracks—sharp, nervous, and wiry—have their histories also. But how rarely we see squirrels in winter! The naturalists say they are mostly torpid; yet evidently that little pocket-faced depredator, the chipmunk, was not carrying buckwheat for so many days to his hole for nothing: was he anticipating a state of torpidity, or providing against the demands of a very active appetite? Red and gray squirrels are more or less active all winter, though very shy, and, I am inclined to think, partially nocturnal in their habits. Here a gray one has just passed,—came down that tree and went up this; there he dug for a beechnut, and left the burr on the snow. How did he know where to dig? During an unusually severe winter I have known him to make long journeys to a barn, in a remote field, where wheat was stored. How did he know there was wheat there? In attempting to return, the adventurous creature was frequently run down and caught in the deep snow.

His home is in the trunk of some old birch or maple, with an entrance far up amid the branches. In the spring he builds himself a summer-house of small leafy twigs in the top of a neighboring beech, where the young are reared and much of the time is passed. But the safer retreat in the maple is not abandoned, and both old and young resort thither in the fall, or when danger threatens. Whether this temporary residence amid the branches is for elegance or pleasure, or for sanitary reasons or domestic convenience, the naturalist has forgotten to mention.

The elegant creature, so cleanly in his habits, so graceful in its carriage, so nimble and daring in its movements, excites feelings of admiration akin to those awakened by the birds and the fairer forms of nature. His passage through the trees is almost a flight. Indeed, the flying squirrel has little or no advantage over him, and in speed and nimbleness cannot compare with him at all. If he miss his footing and fall, he is sure to catch on the next branch; if the connection be broken, he leaps recklessly for the nearest spray or limb, and secures his hold, even if it be by the aid of his teeth.

His career of frolic and festivity begins in the fall, after the birds have left us and the holiday spirit of nature has commenced to subside. How absorbing the pastime of the sportsman who goes to the woods in the still October morning in quest of him! You step lightly across the threshold of the forest, and sit down upon the first log or rock to await the signals. It is so still that the ear suddenly seems to have acquired new powers, and there is no movement to confuse the eye. Presently you hear the rustling of a branch, and see it sway or spring as the squirrel leaps from or to it; or else you hear a disturbance in the dry leaves, and mark one running upon the ground. He has probably seen the intruder, and, not liking his stealthy movements, desires to avoid a nearer acquaintance. Now he mounts a stump to see if the way is clear, then pauses a moment at the foot of a tree to take his bearings, his tail, as he skims along, undulating behind him, and adding to the easy grace and dignity of his movements. Or else you are first advised of his proximity by the dropping of a false nut, or the fragments of the shucks rattling upon the leaves. Or, again, after contemplating you awhile unobserved, and making up his mind that you are not dangerous, he strikes an attitude on a branch, and commences to quack and bark, with an accompanying movement of his tail. Late in the afternoon, when the same stillness reigns, the same scenes are repeated. There is a black variety, quite rare, but mating freely with the gray, from which he seems to be distinguished only in color.

The track of the red squirrel may be known by its smaller size. He is more common and less dignified than the gray, and oftener guilty of petty larceny about the barns and grain-fields. He is most abundant in old barkpeelings, and low, dilapidated hemlocks, from which he makes excursions to the fields and orchards, spinning along the tops of the fences, which afford not only convenient lines of communication, but a safe retreat if danger threatens. He loves to linger about the orchard; and, sitting upright on the topmost stone in the wall, or on the tallest stake in the fence, chipping up an apple for the seeds, his tail conforming to the curve of his back, his paws shifting and turning the apple, he is a pretty sight, and his bright, pert appearance atones for all the mischief he does. At home, in the woods, he is the most frolicsome and loquacious. The appearance of anything unusual, if, after contemplating it a moment, he concludes it not dangerous, excites his unbounded mirth and ridicule, and he snickers and chatters, hardly able to contain himself; now darting up the trunk of a tree and squealing in derision, then hopping into position on a limb and dancing to the music of his own cackle, and all for your special benefit.

There is something very human in this apparent mirth and mockery of the squirrels. It seems to be a sort of ironical laughter, and implies self-conscious pride and exultation in the laugher. "What a ridiculous thing you are, to be sure!" he seems to say; "how clumsy and awkward, and what a poor show for a tail! Look at me, look at me!"—and he capers about in his best style. Again, he would seem to tease you and provoke your attention; then suddenly assumes a tone of good-natured, childlike defiance and derision. That pretty little imp, the chipmunk, will sit on the stone above his den and defy you, as plainly as if he said so, to catch him before he can get into his hole if you can. You hurl a stone at him, and "No you didn't!" comes up from the depth of his retreat.

In February another track appears

upon the snow, slender and delicate, about a third larger than that of the gray squirrel, indicating no haste or speed, but, on the contrary, denoting the most imperturbable ease and leisure, the footprints so close together that the trail appears like a chain of curiously carved links. Sir *Mephitis mephitica,* or, in plain English, the skunk, has awakened from his six weeks' nap, and come out into society again. He is a nocturnal traveler, very bold and impudent, coming quite up to the barn and out-buildings, and sometimes taking up his quarters for the season under the haymow. There is no such word as hurry in his dictionary, as you may see by his path upon the snow. He has a very sneaking, insinuating way, and goes creeping about the fields and woods, never once in a perceptible degree altering his gait, and, if a fence crosses his course, steers for a break or opening to avoid climbing. He is too indolent even to dig his own hole, but appropriates that of a wood-chuck, or hunts out a crevice in the rocks, from which he extends his rambling in all directions, preferring damp, thawy weather. He has very little discretion or cunning, and holds a trap in utter contempt, stepping into it as soon as beside it, relying implicitly for defense against all forms of danger upon the unsavory punishment he is capable of inflicting. He is quite indifferent to both man and beast, and will not hurry himself to get out of the way of either. Walking through the summer fields at twilight, I have come near stepping upon him, and was much the more disturbed of the two. When attacked in the open field he confounds the plans of his enemies by the unheard-of tactics of exposing his rear rather than his front. "Come if you dare," he says, and his attitude makes even the farm-dog pause. After a few encounters of this kind, and if you entertain the usual hostility towards him, your mode of attack will speedily resolve itself into moving about him in a circle, the radius of which will be the exact distance at which you can hurl a stone with accuracy and effect.

He has a secret to keep and knows it, and is careful not to betray himself until he can do so with the most telling effect. I have known him to preserve his serenity even when caught in a steel trap, and look the very picture of injured innocence, manoeuvring carefully and deliberately to extricate his foot from the grasp of the naughty jaws. Do not by any means take pity on him, and lend a helping hand!

How pretty his face and head! How fine and delicate his teeth, like a weasel's or a cat's! When about a third grown, he looks so well that one covets him for a pet. He is quite precocious, however, and capable, even at this tender age, of making a very strong appeal to your sense of smell.

No animal is more cleanly in his habits than he. He is not an awkward boy who cuts his own face with his whip; and neither his flesh nor his fur hints the weapon with which he is armed. The most silent creature known to me, he makes no sound, so far as I have observed, save a diffuse, impatient noise, like that produced by beating your hand with a whisk-broom, when the farm-dog has discovered his retreat in the stone fence. He renders himself obnoxious to the farmer by his partiality for hens' eggs and young poultry. He is a confirmed epicure, and at plundering hen-roosts an expert. Not the full-grown fowls are his victims, but the youngest and most tender. At night Mother Hen receives under her maternal wings a dozen newly hatched chickens, and with much pride and satisfaction feels them all safely tucked away in her feathers. In the morning she is walking about discon-solately, attended by only two or three of all that pretty brood. What has happened? Where are they gone? That pickpocket, Sir Mephitis, could solve the mystery. Quietly has he approached, under cover of darkness, and one by one relieved her of her precious charge. Look closely and you will see their little yellow legs and beaks, or part of a mangled form, lying about on the ground. Or, before the hen has hatched, he may find her out, and, by the same sleight of hand, remove every egg, leaving only the empty blood-stained shells to witness against him. The birds, especially the ground-builders, suffer in like manner from his plundering propensities.

The secretion upon which he relies for defense, and which is the chief source of his unpopularity, while it affords good reasons against cultivating him as a pet, and mars his attractiveness as game, is by no means the greatest indignity that can be offered to a nose. It is a rank, living smell, and has none of the sickening qualities of disease or putrefaction. Indeed, I think a good smeller will enjoy its most refined intensity. It approaches the sublime, and makes the nose tingle. It is tonic and bracing, and, I can readily believe, has rare medicinal qualities. I do not recommend its use as eyewater, though an old farmer assures me it has undoubted virtues when thus applied. Hearing, one night, a disturbance among his hens, he rushed suddenly out to catch the thief, when Sir Mephitis, taken by surprise, and no doubt much annoyed at being interrupted, discharged the vials of his wrath full in the farmer's face, and with such admirable effect that, for a few moments, he was completely blinded, and powerless to revenge himself upon the rogue, who embraced the opportunity to make good his escape; but he declared that afterwards his eyes felt as if purged by fire, and his sight was much clearer.

In March that brief summary of a bear, the raccoon, comes out of his den in the ledges, and leaves his sharp digitigrade track upon the snow,—traveling not unfrequently in pairs,— a lean, hungry couple, bent on pillage and plunder. They have an unenviable time of it,— feasting in the summer and fall, hibernating in winter, and starving in spring. In April I have found the young of the previous year creeping about the fields, so reduced by starvation as to be quite helpless, and offering no resistance to my taking them up by the tail and carrying them home.

The old ones also become very much emaciated, and come boldly up to the barn or other outbuildings in quest of food. I remember, one morning in early spring, of hearing old Cuff, the farm-dog, barking vociferously before it was yet light. When we got up we discovered him, at the foot of an ash-tree standing about thirty rods from the house, looking up at some gray object in the leafless branches, and by his manners and his voice evincing great impatience that we were so tardy in coming to his assistance. Arrived on the spot, we saw in the tree a coon of unusual size. One bold climber proposed to go up and shake him down. This was what old Cuff wanted, and he fairly bounded with delight as he saw his young master shinning up the tree. Approaching within eight or ten feet of the coon, he seized the branch to which it clung and shook long and fiercely. But the coon was in no danger of losing its hold, and, when the climber paused to renew his hold, it turned toward him with a growl, and showed very clearly a purpose to advance to the attack. This caused his pursuer to descend to the ground with all speed. When the coon was finally brought down with a gun, he fought the dog, which was a large, powerful animal, with great fury, returning bite for bite for some moments; and after a quarter of an hour had elapsed and his unequal antagonist had shaken him as a terrier does a rat, making his teeth meet through the small of his back, the coon still showed fight.

They are very tenacious of life, and like the badger will always whip a dog of their own size and weight. A woodchuck can bite severely, having teeth that cut like chisels, but a coon has agility and power of limb as well.

They are considered game only in the fall, or towards the close of summer, when they become fat and their flesh sweet. At this time, cooning in the remote interior is a famous pastime. As this animal is entirely nocturnal in its habits, it is hunted only at night. A piece of corn on some remote side-hill near the mountain, or between two pieces of woods, is most apt to be frequented by them. While the corn is yet green they pull the ears down like hogs, and, tearing open the sheathing of husks, eat the tender, succulent kernels, bruising and destroying much more than they devour. Sometimes their ravages are a matter of serious concern to the farmer. But every such neighborhood has its coon-dog, and the boys and young men dearly love the sport. The party sets out about eight or nine o'clock of a dark, moonless night, and stealthily approaches the cornfield. The dog knows his business, and when he is put into a patch of corn and told to "hunt them up" he makes a thorough search, and will not be misled by any other scent. You hear him rattling through the corn, hither and yon, with great speed. The coons prick up their ears, and leave on the opposite side of the field. In the stillness you may sometimes hear a single stone rattle on the wall as they hurry toward the woods. If the dog finds nothing, he comes back to his master in a short time, and says in his dumb way, "No coon there." But if he strikes a trail, you presently hear a louder rattling on the stone wall, and then a hurried bark as he enters the woods, followed in a few minutes by loud and repeated barking as he reaches the foot of the tree in which the coon has taken refuge. Then follows a pellmell rush of the cooning party up the hill, into the woods, through the brush and the darkness, falling over prostrate trees, pitching into gullies and hollows, losing hats and tearing clothes, till finally, guided by the baying of the faithful dog, the tree is reached. The first thing now in order is to kindle a fire, and, if its light reveals the coon, to shoot him; if not, to fell the tree with an axe. If this happens to be too great a sacrifice of timber and of strength, to sit down at the foot of the tree till morning.

But with March our interest in these phases of animal life, which winter has so emphasized and brought out, begins to decline. Vague rumors are afloat in the air of a great and coming change. We are eager for Winter to be gone, since he, too, is fugitive and cannot keep his place. Invisible hands deface his icy statuary; his chisel has lost its cunning. The drifts, so pure and exquisite, are now earth-stained and weather-worn,—the flutes and scallops, and fine, firm lines, all gone; and what was a grace and an ornament to the hills is now a disfiguration. Like worn and unwashed linen appear the remains of that spotless robe with which he clothed the world as his bride.

But he will not abdicate without a struggle. Day after day he rallies his scattered forces, and night after night pitches his white tents on the hills, and would fain regain his lost ground; but the young prince in every encounter prevails. Slowly and reluctantly the gray old hero retreats up the mountain, till finally the south rain comes in earnest, and in a night he is dead.

Winter Sunshine

50

Burroughs spent many hours reading and writing at his cluttered desk at Slabsides. When he wrote, he didn't use his thumb, holding his stubby pencil between his first two fingers instead. His writing was wavery and nearly illegible.

SPECKLED TROUT

I have been a seeker of trout from my boyhood, and on all the expeditions in which this fish has been the ostensible purpose I have brought home more game than my creel showed. In fact, in my mature years I find I got more of nature into me, more of the woods, the wild, nearer to bird and beast, while threading my native streams for trout, than in almost any other way. It furnished a good excuse to go forth; it pitched one in the right key; it sent one through the fat and marrowy places of field and wood. Then the fisherman has a harmless, preoccupied look; he is a kind of vagrant that nothing fears. He blends himself with the trees and the shadows. All his approaches are gentle and indirect. He times himself to the meandering, soliloquizing stream; its impulse bears him along. At the foot of the waterfall he sits sequestered and hidden in its volume of sound. The birds know he has no designs upon them, and the animals see that his mind is in the creek. His enthusiasm anneals him, and makes him pliable to the scenes and influences he moves among.

Then what acquaintance he makes with the stream! He addresses himself to it as a lover to his mistress; he wooes it and stays with it till he knows its most hidden secrets. It runs through his thoughts not less than through its banks there; he feels the fret and thrust of every bar and boulder. Where it deepens, his purpose deepens; where it is shallow, he is indifferent. He knows how to interpret its every glance and dimple; its beauty haunts him for days.

I am sure I run no risk of overpraising the charm and attractiveness of a well-fed trout stream, every drop of water in it as bright and pure as if the nymphs had brought it all the way from its source in crystal goblets, and as cool as if it had been hatched beneath a glacier. When the heated and soiled and jaded refugee from the city first sees one, he feels as if he would like to turn it into his bosom and let it flow through him a few hours, it suggests such healing freshness and newness. How his roily thoughts would run clear; how the sediment would go downstream! Could he ever have an impure or an unwholesome wish afterward? The next best thing he can do is to tramp along its banks and surrender himself to its influence. If he reads it intently enough, he will, in a measure, be taking it into his mind and heart, and experiencing its salutary ministrations.

Trout streams coursed through every valley my boyhood knew. I crossed them, and was often lured and detained by them, on my way to and from school. We bathed in them during the long summer noons, and felt for the trout under their banks. A holiday was a holiday indeed that brought permission to go fishing over on Rose's Brook, or up Hardscrabble, or in Meeker's Hollow; all-day trips, from morning till night, through meadows and pastures and beechen woods, wherever the shy, limpid stream led. What an appetite it developed! a hunger that was fierce and aboriginal, and that the wild strawberries we plucked as we crossed the hill teased rather than allayed. When but a few hours could be had, gained perhaps by doing some piece of work about the farm or garden in half the allotted time, the little creek that headed in the paternal domain was handy; when half a day was at one's disposal, there were the hemlocks, less than a mile distant, with their loitering, meditative, log-impeded stream and their dusky, fragrant depths. Alert and wide-eyed, one picked his way along, startled now and then by the sudden bursting-up of the partridge, or by the whistling wings of the "dropping snipe," pressing through the brush and the briers, or finding an easy passage over the trunk of a prostrate tree, carefully letting his hook down through some tangle into a still pool, or standing in some high, sombre avenue and watching his line float in and out amid the moss-covered boulders. In my first essayings I used to go to the edge of these hemlocks, seldom dipping into them beyond the first pool where the stream swept under the roots of two large trees. From this point I could look back into the sunlit fields where the cattle were grazing; beyond, all was gloom and mystery; the trout were black, and to my young imagination the silence and the shadows were blacker. But gradually I yielded to the fascination and penetrated the woods farther and farther on each expedition, till the heart of the mystery was fairly plucked out. During the second or third year of my piscatorial experience I went through them, and through the pasture and meadow beyond, and through another strip of hemlocks, to where the little stream joined the main creek of the valley.

In June, when my trout fever ran pretty high, and an auspicious day arrived, I would make a trip to a stream a couple of miles distant, that came down out of a comparatively new settlement. It was a rapid mountain brook presenting many difficult problems to the young angler, but a very enticing stream for all that, with its two sawmill dams, its pretty cascades, its high, shelving rocks sheltering the mossy nests of the phoebe-bird, and its general wild and forbidding aspects.

But a meadow brook was always a favorite. The trout like meadows; doubtless their food is more abundant there, and, usually, the good hiding-places are more numerous. As soon as you strike a meadow the character of the creek changes: it goes slower and lies deeper; it tarries to enjoy the high, cool banks and to half hide beneath them; it loves the willows, or rather the willows love it and shelter it from the sun; its spring runs are kept cool by the overhanging grass, and the heavy turf that faces its open banks is not cut away by the sharp hoofs of the grazing cattle. Then there are the bobolinks and the starlings and

the meadowlarks, always interested spectators of the angler; there are also the marsh marigolds, the buttercups, or the spotted lilies, and the good angler is always an interested spectator of them. In fact, the patches of meadow land that lie in the angler's course are like the happy experiences in his own life, or like the fine passages in the poem he is reading; the pasture oftener contains the shallow and monotonous places. In the small streams the cattle scare the fish, and soil their element and break down their retreats under the banks. Woodland alternates the best with meadow: the creek loves to burrow under the roots of a great tree, to scoop out a pool after leaping over the prostrate trunk of one, and to pause at the foot of a ledge of moss-covered rocks, with ice-cold water dripping down. How straight the current goes for the rock! Note its corrugated, muscular appearance; it strikes and glances off, but accumulates, deepens with well-defined eddies above and to one side; on the edge of these the trout lurk and spring upon their prey.

The angler learns that it is generally some obstacle or hindrance that makes a deep place in the creek, as in a brave life; and his ideal brook is one that lies in deep, well-defined banks, yet makes many a shift from right to left, meets with many rebuffs and adventures, hurled back upon itself by rocks, waylaid by snags and trees, tripped up by precipices, but sooner or later reposing under meadow banks, deepening and eddying beneath bridges, or prosperous and strong in some level stretch of cultivated land with great elms shading it here and there.

But I early learned that from almost any stream in a trout country the true angler could take trout, and that the great secret was this, that, whatever bait you used, worm, grasshopper, grub, or fly, there was one thing you must always put upon your hook, namely, your heart: when you bait your hook with your heart the fish always bite; they will jump clear from the water after it; they will dispute with each other over it; it is a morsel they love above everything else. With such bait I have seen the born angler (my grandfather was one) take a noble string of trout from the most unpromising waters, and on the most unpromising day. He used his hook so coyly and tenderly, he approached the fish with such address and insinuation, he divined the exact spot where they lay: if they were not eager, he humored them and seemed to steal by them; if they were playful and coquettish, he would suit his mood to theirs; if they were frank and sincere, he met them halfway; he was so patient and considerate, so entirely devoted to pleasing the critical trout, and so successful in his efforts,—surely his heart was upon his hook, and it was a tender, unctuous heart, too, as that of every angler is. How nicely he would measure the distance! how dexterously he would avoid an overhanging limb or bush and drop the line exactly in the right spot! Of course there was a pulse of feeling and sympathy to the extremity of that line. If your heart is a stone, however, or an empty husk, there is no use to put it upon your hook; it will not tempt the fish; the bait must be quick and fresh. Indeed, a certain quality of youth is indispensable to the successful angler, a certain unworldliness and readiness to invest yourself in an enterprise that doesn't pay in the current coin. Not only is the angler, like the poet, born and not made, as Walton says, but there is a deal of the poet in him, and he is to be judged no more harshly; he is the victim of his genius: those wild streams, how they haunt him! he will play truant to dull care, and flee to them; their waters impart somewhat of their own perpetual youth to him. My grandfather when he was eighty years old would take down his pole as eagerly as any boy, and step off with wonderful elasticity toward the beloved streams; it used to try my young legs a good deal to follow him, specially on the return trip. And no poet was ever more innocent of worldly success or ambition. For, to paraphrase Tennyson,—

> "Lusty trout to him were scrip and share,
> And babbling waters more than cent for cent."

He laid up treasures, but they were not in this world. In fact, though the kindest of husbands, I fear he was not what the country people call a "good provider," except in providing trout in their season, though it is doubtful if there was always fat in the house to fry them in. But he could tell you they were worse off than that at Valley Forge, and that trout, or any other fish, were good roasted in the ashes under the coals. He had the Walton requisite of loving quietness and contemplation, and was devout withal. Indeed, in many ways he was akin to those Galilee fishermen who were called to be fishers of men. How he read the Book and pored over it, even at times, I suspect, nodding over it, and laying it down only to take up his rod, over which, unless the trout were very dilatory and the journey very fatiguing, he never nodded!

Locusts and Wild Honey

Like his maternal grandfather, Edmund Kelly, Burroughs was a dedicated seeker of trout all his life. This expedition was to Esopus Creek, a stream near Riverby.

The matchless old blue sky again from the west—the gift of a high barometer. The peculiar blue of the sky, a translucent blue—not the color of *something*, but of empty space—an unfading, immortal blue. As Homer and the prophets saw it, *we* see it to-day.

The Heart of Burroughs's Journals

Blue sky in the west all day. The first blue sky that appeared above the earth—think of it! There must have been a time when the vapors above the earth opened and let the blue sky shine through for the first time. The primal bad spell of weather was clearing up.

The Heart of Burroughs's Journals

When varied tints outline the trees,
Like figures sketched upon a screen,
And all the forest shows degrees
Of tawny red and yellow-green;

When purple finches sing and soar,
Then drop to perch on open wing,
With vernal gladness running o'er—
The feathered lyrist of the spring:

When joys like these salute the sense,
And bloom and perfume fill the day,
Then waiting long hath recompense,
And all the world is glad with May.

Bird and Bough

Woe to any artist who disengages Beauty from the wide background of rudeness, darkness, and strength,—and disengages her from absolute nature! The mild and beneficent aspects of nature,—what gulfs and abysses of power underlie them! The great shaggy, barbaric earth,—yet the summing-up, the plenum, of all we know or can know of beauty! So the orbic poems of the world have a foundation as of the earth itself, and are beautiful because they are something else first.

Birds and Poets

Nearly every season I make the acquaintance of one or more new flowers. It takes years to exhaust the botanical treasures of any one considerable neighborhood, unless one makes a dead set at it, like an herbalist. One likes to have his floral acquaintances come to him easily and naturally, like his other friends. Some pleasant occasion should bring you together. You meet in a walk, or touch elbows on a picnic under a tree, or get acquainted on a fishing or camping-out expedition. What comes to you in the way of birds or flowers, while wooing only the large spirit of open-air nature, seems like special good fortune. At any rate, one does not want to bolt his botany, but rather to prolong the course. One likes to have something in reserve, something to be on the look-out for on his walks.

Riverby

Days of great freshness and beauty. A sort of luminous greenness everywhere; the young leaves seem to let the light through them—a green transparency. The youth of Nature, when we almost see the blood in her veins, her integument is yet so delicate and thin.

The Heart of Burroughs's Journals

I know of nothing in vegetable nature that seems so really to be *born* as the ferns. They emerge from the ground rolled up, with a rudimentary and "touch-me-not" look, and appear to need a maternal tongue to lick them into shape. The sun plays the wet-nurse to them, and very soon they are out of that uncanny covering in which they come swathed, and take their places with other green things.

Signs and Seasons

Solitude is not for the young; the young have no thoughts or experiences, but only unsatisfied desires; it is for the middle-aged and the old, for a man when he has ripened and wants time to mellow his thoughts. A man who retires into solitude must have a capital of thought and experience to live upon, or his soul will perish of want.

Indoor Studies

A YOUNG MARSH HAWK

Most country boys, I fancy, know the marsh hawk. It is he you see flying low over the fields, beating about bushes and marshes and dipping over the fences, with his attention directed to the ground beneath him. He is a cat on wings. He keeps so low that the birds and mice do not see him till he is fairly upon them. The hen-hawk swoops down upon the meadow-mouse from his position high in air, or from the top of a dead tree; but the marsh hawk stalks him and comes suddenly upon him from over the fence, or from behind a low bush or tuft of grass. He is nearly as large as the hen-hawk, but has a much longer tail. When I was a boy, I used to call him the long-tailed hawk. The male is a bluish slate color; the female a reddish brown, like the hen-hawk, with a white rump.

Unlike the other hawks, they nest on the ground in low, thick marshy places. For several seasons a pair have nested in a bushy marsh a few miles back of me, near the house of a farmer friend of mine, who has a keen eye for the wild life about him. Two years ago he found the nest, but when I got over to see it the next week, it had been robbed, probably by some boys in the neighborhood. The past season, in April or May, by watching the mother bird, he found the nest again. It was in a marshy place, several acres in extent, in the bottom of a valley, and thickly grown with hardhack, prickly ash, smilax, and other low thorny bushes. My friend brought me to the brink of a low hill, and pointed out to me in the marsh below us, as nearly as he could, just where the nest was located. Then we crossed the pasture, entered upon the marsh, and made our way cautiously toward it. The wild thorny growths, waist high, had to be carefully dealt with. As we neared the spot, I used my eyes the best I could, but I did not see the hawk till she sprang into the air not ten yards away from us. She went screaming upward, and was soon sailing in a circle far above us. There, on a coarse matting of twigs and weeds, lay five snow-white eggs, a little more than half as large as hens' eggs. My companion said the male hawk would probably soon appear and join the female, but he did not. She kept drifting away to the east, and was soon gone from our sight.

We soon withdrew and secreted ourselves behind the stone wall, in hopes of seeing the mother hawk return. She appeared in the distance, but seemed to know she was being watched, and kept away. About ten days later we made another visit to the nest. An adventurous young Chicago lady also wanted to see a hawk's nest, and so accompanied us. This time three of the eggs were hatched, and as the mother hawk sprang up, either by accident or intentionally, she threw two of the young hawks some feet from the nest. She rose up and screamed angrily. Then, turning toward us, she came like an arrow straight at the young lady, a bright plume in whose hat probably drew her fire. The damsel gathered up her skirts about her and beat a hasty retreat. Hawks were not so pretty as she thought they were. A large hawk launched at one's face from high in the air is calculated to make one a little nervous. It is such a fearful incline down which the bird comes, and she is aiming exactly toward your eye. When within about thirty feet of you, she turns upward with a rushing sound, and, mounting higher, falls toward you again. She is only firing blank cartridges, as it were; but it usually has the desired effect, and beats the enemy off.

After we had inspected the young hawks, a neighbor of my friend offered to conduct us to a quail's nest. Anything in the shape of a nest is always welcome, it is such a mystery, such a centre of interest and affection, and, if upon the ground, is usually something so dainty and exquisite amid the natural wreckage and confusion. A ground-nest seems so exposed, too, that it always gives a little thrill of pleasurable surprise to see the group of frail eggs resting there behind so slight a barrier. I will walk a long distance any day just to see a song sparrow's nest amid the stubble or under a tuft of grass. It is a jewel in a rosette of jewels, with a frill of weeds or turf. A quail's nest I had never seen, and to be shown one within the hunting-ground of this murderous hawk would be a double pleasure. Such a quiet, secluded, grass-grown highway as we moved along was itself a rare treat. Sequestered was the word that the little valley suggested, and peace the feeling the road evoked. The farmer, whose fields lay about us, half grown with weeds and bushes, evidently did not make stir or noise enough to disturb anything. Beside this rustic highway, bounded by old mossy stone walls, and within a stone's throw of the farmer's barn, the quail had made her nest. It was just under the edge of a prostrate thorn-bush.

"The nest is right there," said the farmer, pausing within ten feet of it, and pointing to the spot with his stick.

In a moment or two we could make out the mottled brown plumage of the sitting bird. Then we approached her cautiously till we bent above her.

She never moved a feather.

Then I put my cane down in the brush behind her. We wanted to see the eggs, yet did not want rudely to disturb the sitting hen.

She would not move.

Then I put down my hand within a few inches of her; still she kept her place. Should we have to lift her off bodily?

Then the young lady put down her hand, probably the prettiest and the whitest hand the quail had ever seen. At least it started her, and off she sprang, uncovering such a crowded nest of eggs as I had never before beheld. Twenty-one of them! a ring or disk of white like a china tea-saucer. You could not help saying How pretty! How cunning! like baby hens' eggs, as if the bird were playing at sitting as children play at housekeeping.

If I had known how crowded her nest was, I should not have dared disturb her, for fear she would break some of them. But not an egg suffered harm by her sudden flight; and no harm came to the nest afterward. Every egg hatched, I was told, and the little chicks, hardly bigger than bumblebees, were led away by the mother into the fields.

In about a week I paid another visit to the hawk's nest. The eggs were all hatched, and the mother bird was hovering near. I shall never forget the curious expression of those young hawks sitting there on the ground. The expression was not one of youth, but of extreme age. Such an ancient, infirm look as they had,—the sharp, dark, and shrunken look about the face and eyes, and their feeble, tottering motions! They sat upon their elbows and the hind part of their bodies, and their pale, withered legs and feet extended before them in the most helpless fashion. Their angular bodies were covered with a pale yellowish down, like that of a chicken; their heads had a plucked, seedy appearance; and their long, strong, naked wings hung down by their sides till they touched the ground: power and ferocity in the first rude draught, shorn of everything but its sinister ugliness. Another curious thing was the gradation of the young in size; they tapered down regularly from the first to the fifth, as if there had been, as probably there was, an interval of a day or two between the hatchings.

The two older ones showed some signs of fear on our approach, and one of them threw himself upon his back, and put up his impotent legs, and glared at us with open beak. The two smaller ones regarded us not at all. Neither of the parent birds appeared during our stay.

When I visited the nest again, eight or ten days later, the birds were much grown, but of as marked a difference in size as before, and with the same look of extreme old age,—old age in men of the aquiline type, nose and chin coming together, and eyes large and sunken. They now glared upon us with a wild, savage look, and opened their beaks threateningly.

The next week, when my friend visited the nest, the larger of the hawks fought him savagely. But one of the brood, probably the last to hatch, had made but little growth. It appeared to be on the point of starvation. The mother hawk (for the male seemed to have disappeared) had perhaps found her family too large for her, and was deliberately allowing one of the number to perish; or did the larger and stronger young devour all the food before the weaker member could obtain any? Probably this was the case.

Arthur brought the feeble nestling away, and the same day my little boy got it and brought it home, wrapped in a woolen rag. It was clearly a starved bantling. It cried feebly, but would not lift up its head.

We first poured some warm milk down its throat, which soon revived it, so that it would swallow small bits of flesh. In a day or two we had it eating ravenously, and its growth became noticeable. Its voice had the sharp whistling character of that of its parents, and was stilled only when the bird was asleep. We made a pen for it, about a yard square, in one end of the study, covering the floor with several thicknesses of newspapers; and here, upon a bit of brown woolen blanket for a nest, the hawk waxed strong day by day. An uglier-looking pet, tested by all

the rules we usually apply to such things, would have been hard to find. There he would sit upon his elbows, his helpless feet out in front of him, his great featherless wings touching the floor, and shrilly cry for more food. For a time we gave him water daily from a stylograph-pen filler, but the water he evidently did not need or relish. Fresh meat, and plenty of it, was his demand. And we soon discovered that he liked game, such as mice, squirrels, birds, much better than butcher's meat.

Then began a lively campaign on the part of my little boy against all the vermin and small game in the neighborhood, to keep the hawk supplied. He trapped and he hunted, he enlisted his mates in his service, he even robbed the cats to feed the hawk. His usefulness as a boy of all work was seriously impaired. "Where is J—?" "Gone after a squirrel for his hawk." And often the day would be half gone before his hunt was successful. The premises were very soon cleared of mice, and the vicinity of chipmunks and squirrels. Farther and farther he was compelled to hunt the surrounding farms and woods to keep up with the demands of the hawk. By the time the hawk was ready to fly, he had consumed twenty-one chipmunks, fourteen red squirrels, sixteen mice, and twelve English sparrows, besides a lot of butcher's meat.

His plumage very soon began to show itself, crowding off tufts of the down. The quills on his great wings sprouted and grew apace. What a ragged, uncanny appearance he presented! but his look of extreme age gradually became modified. What a lover of the sunlight he was! We would put him out upon the grass in the full blaze of the morning sun, and he would spread his wings and bask in it with the most intense enjoyment. In the nest the young must be exposed to the full power of the midday sun during our first heated terms in June and July, the thermometer often going up to ninety-three or ninety-five degrees, so that sunshine seemed to be a need of his nature. He liked the rain equally well, and when put out in a shower would sit down and take it as if every drop did him good.

His legs developed nearly as slowly as his wings. He could not stand steadily upon them till about ten days before he was ready to fly. The talons were limp and feeble. When we came with food, he would hobble along toward us like the worst kind of a cripple, drooping and moving his wings, and treading upon his legs from the foot back to the elbow, the foot remaining closed and useless. Like a baby learning to stand, he made many trials before he succeeded. He would rise up on his trembling legs only to fall back again.

One day, in the summer-house, I saw him for the first time stand for a moment squarely upon his legs with the feet fully spread beneath them. He looked about him as if the world suddenly wore a new aspect.

His plumage now grew quite rapidly. One red squirrel a day, chopped fine with an axe, was his ration. He began to hold his game with his foot while he tore it. The study was full of his shed down. His dark brown mottled plumage began to grow beautiful. The wings drooped a little, but gradually he got control of them, and held them in place.

It was now the 20th of July, and the hawk was about five weeks old. In a day or two he was walking or jumping about the ground. He chose a position under the edge of a Norway spruce, where he would sit for hours dozing, or looking out upon the landscape. When we brought him game, he would advance to meet us with wings slightly lifted, and uttering a shrill cry. Toss him a mouse or sparrow, and he would seize it with one foot and hop off to his cover, where he would bend above it, spread his plumage, look this way and that, uttering all the time the most exultant and satisfied chuckle.

About this time he began to practice striking with his talons, as an Indian boy might begin practicing with his bow and arrow. He would strike at a dry leaf in the grass, or at a fallen apple, or at some imaginary object. He was learning the use of his weapons. His wings also,—he seemed to feel them sprouting from his shoulders. He would lift them straight up and hold them expanded, and they would seem to quiver with excitement. Every hour in the day he would do this. The pressure was beginning to centre there. Then he would strike playfully at a leaf or a bit of wood, and keep his wings lifted.

The next step was to spring into the air and beat his wings. He seemed now to be thinking entirely of his wings. They itched to be put to use.

A day or two later he would leap and fly several feet. A pile of brush ten or twelve feet below the bank was easily reached. Here he would perch in true hawk fashion, to the bewilderment and scandal of all the robins and catbirds in the vicinity. Here he would dart his eye in all directions, turning his head over and glancing up into the sky.

He was now a lovely creature, fully fledged, and as tame as a kitten. But he was not a bit like a kitten in one respect,—he could not bear to have you stroke or even touch his plumage. He had a horror of your hand, as if it would hopelessly defile him. But he would perch upon it, and allow you to carry him about. If a dog or cat appeared, he was ready to give battle instantly. He rushed up to a little dog one day, and struck him with his foot savagely. He was afraid of strangers, and of any unusual object.

The last week in July he began to fly quite freely, and it was necessary to clip one of his wings. As the clipping embraced only the ends of his primaries, he soon overcame the difficulty, and by carrying his broad, long tail more on that side, flew with considerable ease. He made longer and longer excursions into the surrounding fields and vineyards, and did not always return. On such occasions we would go find him and fetch him back.

Late one rainy afternoon he flew away into the vineyard, and when, an hour later, I went after him, he could not be found, and we never saw him again. We hoped hunger would soon drive him back, but we have had no clew to him from that day to this.

Riverby

Burroughs was a frequent visitor to Black Creek. He read and meditated along its banks, hunted and fished on its waters. He took Walt Whitman to see a falls on the stream in 1879, and thereafter proudly pointed out to other guests the spot where the poet sat.

BIRDS'-NESTING

Birds'-nesting is by no means a failure, even though you find no birds'-nests. You are sure to find other things of interest, plenty of them. A friend of mine says that, in his youth, he used to go hunting with his gun loaded for wild turkeys, and, though he frequently saw plenty of smaller game, he generally came home empty-handed, because he was loaded only for turkeys. But the student of ornithology, who is also a lover of Nature in all her shows and forms, does not go out loaded for turkeys merely, but for everything that moves or grows, and is quite sure, therefore, to bag some game, if not with his gun, then with his eye, or his nose, or his ear. Even a crow's nest is not amiss, or a den in the rocks where the coons or the skunks live, or a log where a partridge drums, or the partridge himself starting up with spread tail, and walking a few yards in advance of you before he goes humming through the woods, or a woodchuck hole, with well beaten and worn entrance, and with the saplings gnawed and soiled about it, or the strong, fetid smell of the fox, which a sharp nose detects here and there, and which is a good perfume in the woods. And then it is enough to come upon a spring in the woods and stoop down and drink of the sweet, cold water, and bathe your hands in it, or to walk along a trout brook, which has absorbed the shadows till it has itself become but a denser shade. Then I am always drawn out of my way by a ledge of rocks, and love nothing better than to explore the caverns and dens, or to sit down under the overhanging crags and let the wild scene absorb me.

There is a fascination about ledges! They are an unmistakable feature, and give emphasis and character to the scene. I feel their spell, and must pause awhile. Time, old as the hills and older, looks out of their scarred and weather-worn face. The woods are of to-day, but the ledges, in comparison, are of eternity. One pokes about them as he would about ruins, and with something of the same feeling. They are ruins of the fore world. Here the foundations of the hills were laid; here the earth-giants wrought and builded. They constrain one to silence and meditation; the whispering and rustling trees seem trivial and impertinent.

And then there are birds'-nests about ledges, too, exquisite mossy tenements, with white, pebbly eggs, that I can never gaze upon without emotion. The little brown bird, the phoebe, looks at you from her niche till you are within a few feet of her, when she darts away. Occasionally you may find the nest of some rare wood-warbler forming a little pocket in the apron of moss that hangs down over the damp rocks.

The sylvan folk seem to know when you are on a peaceful mission, and are less afraid than usual. Did not that marmot to-day guess that my errand did not concern him as he saw me approach from his cover in the bushes? But when he saw me pause and deliberately seat myself on the stone wall immediately over his hole, his confidence was much shaken. He apparently deliberated awhile, for I heard the leaves rustle as if he were making up his mind, when he suddenly broke cover and came for his hole full tilt. Any other animal would have taken to his heels and fled; but a woodchuck's heels do not amount to much for speed, and he feels his only safety is in his hole. On he came in the most obstinate and determined manner, and I dare say if I had sat down in his hole, would have attacked me unhesitatingly. This I did not give him a chance to do; but, not to be entirely outdone, attempted to set my feet on him in no very gentle manner; but he whipped into his den beneath me with a defiant snort. Farther on, a saucy chipmunk presumed upon my harmless character to an unwonted degree also. I had paused to bathe my hands and face in a little trout brook, and had set a tin cup, which I had partly filled with strawberries as I crossed the field, on a stone at my feet, when along came the chipmunk as confidently as if he knew precisely where he was going, and, perfectly oblivious of my presence, cocked himself up on the rim of the cup and proceeded to eat my choicest berries. I remained motionless and observed him. He had eaten but two when the thought seemed to occur to him that he might be doing better, and he began to fill his pockets. Two, four, six, eight of my berries quickly disappeared, and the cheeks of the little vagabond swelled. But all the time he kept eating, that not a moment might be lost. Then he hopped off the cup, and went skipping from stone to stone till the brook was passed, when he disappeared in the woods. In two or three minutes he was back again, and went to stuffing himself as before; then he disappeared a second time, and I imagined told a friend of his, for in a moment or two along came a bobtailed chipmunk, as if in search of something, and passed up, and down, and around, but did not quite hit the spot. Shortly, the first returned a third time, and had now grown a little fastidious, for he began to sort over my berries, and to bite into them, as if to taste their quality. He was not long in loading up, however, and in making off again. But I had now got tired of the joke, and my berries were appreciably diminishing, so I moved away. What was most curious about the proceeding was, that the little poacher took different directions each time, and returned from different ways. Was this to elude pursuit, or was he distributing the fruit to his friends and neighbors about, astonishing them with strawberries for lunch?

But I am making slow headway toward finding the birds'-nests, for I had set out on this occasion in hopes of finding a rare nest,—the nest of the black-throated blue-backed warbler, which, it seemed, with one or two others, was still wanting to make the history of our warblers complete. The woods were extensive, and full of deep, dark tangles, and looking for any particular nest seemed about as hopeless a task as searching for a needle in a haystack, as the old saying is. Where to begin, and how? But the principle is the same as in looking for a hen's nest,—first find your bird, then watch its movements.

The bird is in these woods, for I have seen him scores of times, but whether he builds high or low, on the ground or in the trees, is all unknown to me. That is his song now,—"twe-twea-twe-e-e-a," with a peculiar summer languor and plaintiveness, and issuing from the lower branches and growths. Presently we—for I have been joined by a companion—discover the bird, a male, insecting in the top of a newly fallen hemlock. The black, white, and blue of his uniform are seen at a glance. His movements are quite slow compared with some of the warblers. If he will only betray the locality of that little domicile where his plainly clad mate is evidently sitting, it is all we will ask of him. But this he seems in no wise disposed to do. Here and there, and up and down, we follow him, often losing him, and as often refinding him by his song; but the clew to his nest, how shall we get it? Does he never go home to see how things are getting on, or to see if his presence is not needed, or to take madam a morsel of food? No doubt he keeps within earshot, and a cry of distress or alarm from the mother bird would bring him to the spot in an instant. Would that some evil fate would make her cry, then! Presently he encounters a rival. His feeding-ground infringes upon that of another, and the two birds regard each other threateningly. This is a good sign, for their nests are evidently near.

Their battle-cry is a low, peculiar chirp, not very fierce, but bantering and confident. They quickly come to blows, but it is a very fantastic battle, and, as it would seem, indulged in more to satisfy their sense of honor than to hurt each other, for neither party gets the better of the other, and they separate a few paces and sing, and squeak, and challenge each other in a very happy frame of mind. The gauntlet is no sooner thrown down than it is again taken up by one or the other, and in the course of fifteen or twenty minutes they have three or four encounters, separating a little, then provoked to return again like two cocks, till finally they withdraw beyond hearing of each other,—both, no doubt, claiming the victory. But the secret of the nest is still kept. Once I think I have it. I catch a glimpse of a bird which looks like the female, and near by, in a small hemlock about eight feet from the ground, my eye detects a nest. But as I come up under it, I can see daylight through it, and that it is empty,—evidently only part finished, not lined or padded yet. Now if the bird will only return and claim it, the point will be gained. But we wait and watch in vain. The architect has knocked off to-day, and we must come again, or continue our search.

While loitering about here we were much amused by three chipmunks, who seemed to be engaged in some kind of game. It looked very much as if they were playing tag. Round and round they would go, first one taking the lead, then another, all good-natured and gleeful as schoolboys. There is one thing about a chipmunk that is peculiar: he is never more than one jump from home. Make a dive at him anywhere and in he goes. He knows where the hole is, even when it is covered up with leaves. There is no doubt, also, that he has his own sense of humor and fun, as what squirrel has not? I have watched two red squirrels for a half hour coursing through the large trees by the roadside where branches interlocked, and engaged in a game of tag as obviously as two boys. As soon as the pursuer had come up with the pursued, and actually touched him, the palm was his, and away he would go, taxing his wits and his speed to the utmost to elude his fellow.

Despairing of finding either of the nests of the two males, we pushed on through the woods to try our luck elsewhere. Before long, just as we were about to plunge down a hill into a dense, swampy part of the woods, we discovered a pair of the birds we were in quest of. They had food in their beaks, and, as we paused, showed great signs of alarm, indicating that the nest was in the immediate vicinity. This was enough. We would pause here and find this nest, anyhow. To make a sure thing of it, we determined to watch the parent birds till we had wrung from them their secret. So we doggedly crouched down and watched them, and they watched us. It was diamond cut diamond. But as we felt constrained in our movements, desiring, if possible, to keep so quiet that the birds would, after a while, see in us only two harmless stumps or prostrate logs, we had much the worst of it. The mosquitoes were quite taken with our quiet, and knew us from logs and stumps in a moment. Neither were the birds deceived, not even when we tried the Indian's tactics, and plumed ourselves with green branches. Ah, the suspicious creatures, how they watched us with the food in their beaks, abstaining for one whole hour from ministering that precious charge which otherwise would have been visited every moment! Quite near us they would come at times, between us and the nest, eying us so sharply. Then they would move off, and apparently try to forget our presence. Was it to deceive us, or to persuade himself and mate that there was no serious cause for alarm, that the male would now and then strike up in full song and move off to some distance through the trees? But the mother bird did not allow herself to lose sight of us at all, and both birds, after carrying the food in their beaks a long time, would swallow it themselves. Then they would obtain another morsel and apparently approach very near the nest, when their caution or prudence would come to their aid, and they would swallow the food and hasten away. I thought the young birds would cry out, but not a syllable from them. Yet this was, no doubt, what kept the parent birds away from the nest. The clamor the young would have set up on the approach of the old with food would have exposed everything.

After a time I felt sure I knew within a few feet where the nest was concealed. Indeed, I thought I knew the identical bush. Then the birds approached each other again and grew very confidential about another locality some rods below. This puzzled us, and, seeing the whole afternoon might be spent in this manner, and the mystery unsolved, we determined to change our tactics and institute a thorough search of the locality. This procedure soon brought things to a crisis, for, as my companion clambered over a log by a little hemlock, a few yards from where we had been sitting, with a cry of alarm out sprang the young birds from their nest in the hemlock, and, scampering and fluttering over the leaves, disappeared in different directions. This brought the parent birds on the scene in an agony of alarm. Their distress was pitiful. They threw themselves on the ground at our very feet, and fluttered, and cried, and trailed themselves before us, to draw us away from the place, or distract our attention from the helpless young. I shall not forget the male bird, how bright he looked, how sharp the contrast as he trailed his painted plumage there on the dry leaves. Apparently he was seriously disabled. He would start up as if exerting every muscle to fly away, but no use; down he would come, with a helpless, fluttering motion, before he had gone two yards, and apparently you had only to go and pick him up. But before you could pick him up, he had recovered somewhat and flown a little farther; and thus, if you were tempted to follow him, you would soon find yourself some distance from the scene of the nest, and both old and young well out of your

reach. The female bird was not less solicitous, and practiced the same arts upon us to decoy us away, but her dull plumage rendered her less noticeable. The male was clad in holiday attire, but his mate in an every-day working-garb.

The nest was built in the fork of a little hemlock, about fifteen inches from the ground, and was a thick, firm structure, composed of the finer material of the woods, with a lining of very delicate roots or rootlets. There were four young birds and one addled egg. We found it in a locality about the head-waters of the eastern branch of the Delaware, where several other of the rarer species of warblers, such as the mourning ground, the Blackburnian, the chestnut-sided, and the speckled Canada, spend the summer and rear their young.

Defunct birds'-nests are easy to find; when the leaves fall, then they are in every bush and tree; and one wonders how he missed them; but a live nest, how it eludes one! I have read of a noted criminal who could hide himself pretty effectually in any room that contained the usual furniture; he would embrace the support of a table so as to seem part of it. The bird has studied the same art: it always blends its nest with the surroundings, and sometimes its very openness hides it; the light itself seems to conceal it. Then the birds build anew each year, and so always avail themselves of the present and latest combination of leaves and screens, of light and shade. What was very well concealed one season may be quite exposed the next.

Going a-fishing or a-berrying is a good introduction to the haunts of the birds, and to their nesting-places. You put forth your hand for the berries, and there is a nest; or your tread by the creeks starts the sandpiper or the water-thrush from the ground where its eggs are concealed, or some shy wood-warbler from a bush. One day, fishing down a deep wooded gorge, my hook caught on a limb overhead, and on pulling it down I found I had missed my trout, but had caught a hummingbird's nest. It was saddled on the limb as nicely as if it had been a grown part of it.

Other collectors beside the oologists are looking for birds'-nests,—the squirrels and owls and jays and crows. The worst depredator in this direction I know of is the fish crow, and I warn him to keep off my premises, and charge every gunner to spare him not. He is a small sneak-thief, and will rob the nest of every robin, wood thrush, and oriole he can come at. I believe he fishes only when he is unable to find birds' eggs or young birds. The genuine crow, the crow with the honest "caw," "caw," I have never caught in such small business, though the kingbird makes no discrimination between them, but accuses both alike.

Locusts and Wild Honey

On July 10, 1903, the President and Mrs. Theodore Roosevelt called on Burroughs and hiked up to Slabsides. Mrs. Burroughs served one of her famous huckleberry pies, and Julian photographed his father and the distinguished guests. Roosevelt called Burroughs "Oom John" and dedicated a book to him; Burroughs called Roosevelt "His Transparency" and was deeply touched by the President's friendship.

THE CHIPMUNK

The first chipmunk in March is as sure a token of the spring as the first bluebird or the first robin; and it is quite as welcome. Some genial influence has found him out there in his burrow, deep under the ground, and waked him up, and enticed him forth into the light of day. The red squirrel has been more or less active all winter; his track has dotted the surface of every new-fallen snow throughout the season. But the chipmunk retired from view early in December, and has passed the rigorous months in his nest, beside his hoard of nuts, some feet underground, and hence, when he emerges in March, and is seen upon his little journeys along the fences, or perched upon a log or rock near his hole in the woods, it is another sign that spring is at hand. His store of nuts may or may not be all consumed; it is certain that he is no sluggard, to sleep away these first bright warm days.

Before the first crocus is out of the ground, you may look for the first chipmunk. When I hear the little downy woodpecker begin his spring drumming, then I know the chipmunk is due. He cannot sleep after that challenge of the woodpecker reaches his ear.

Apparently the first thing he does on coming forth, as soon as he is sure of himself, is to go courting. So far as I have observed, the love-making of the chipmunk occurs in March. A single female will attract all the males in the vicinity. One early March day I was at work for several hours near a stone fence, where a female had apparently taken up her quarters. What a train of suitors she had that day! how they hurried up and down, often giving each other a spiteful slap or bite as they passed. The young are born in May, four or five at a birth.

The chipmunk is quite a solitary creature; I have never known more than one to occupy the same den. Apparently no two can agree to live together. What a clean, pert, dapper, nervous little fellow he is! How fast his heart beats, as he stands up on the wall by the roadside, and, with hands spread out upon his breast, regards you intently! A movement of your arm, and he darts into the wall with a saucy *chip-r-r*, which has the effect of slamming the door behind him.

On some still day in autumn, the nutty days, the woods will often be pervaded by an undertone of sound, produced by their multitudinous clucking, as they sit near their dens. It is one of the characteristic sounds of fall.

The chipmunk has many enemies, such as cats, weasels, black snakes, hawks, and owls. One season one had his den in the side of the bank near my study. As I stood regarding his goings and comings, one October morning, I saw him, when a few yards away from his hole, turn and retreat with all speed. As he darted beneath the sod, a shrike swooped down and hovered a moment on the wing just over the hole where he had disappeared. I doubt if the shrike could have killed him, but it certainly gave him a good fright.

It was amusing to watch this chipmunk carry nuts and other food into his den. He had made a well-defined path from his door out through the weeds and dry leaves into the territory where his feeding-ground lay. The path was a crooked one; it dipped under weeds, under some large, loosely piled stones, under a pile of chestnut posts, and then followed the remains of an old wall. Going and coming, his motions were like clockwork. He always went by spurts and sudden sallies. He was never for one moment off his guard. He would appear at the mouth of his den, look quickly about, take a few leaps to a tussock of grass, pause a breath with one foot raised, slip quickly a few yards over some dry leaves, pause again by a stump beside a path, rush across the path to the pile of loose stones, go under the first and over the second, gain the pile of posts, make his way through that, survey his course a half moment from the other side of it, and then dart on to some other cover, and presently beyond my range, where I think he gathered acorns, as there were no other nut-bearing trees than oaks near. In four or five minutes I would see him coming back, always keeping rigidly to the course he took going out, pausing at the same spots, darting over or under the same objects, clearing at a bound the same pile of leaves. There was no variation in his manner of proceeding all the time I observed him.

He was alert, cautious, and exceedingly methodical. He had found safety in a certain course, and he did not at any time deviate a hair's breadth from it. Something seemed to say to him all the time, "Beware, beware!" The nervous, impetuous ways of these creatures are no doubt the result of the life of fear which they lead.

My chipmunk had no companion. He lived all by himself in true hermit fashion, as is usually the case with this squirrel. Provident creature that he is, one would think that he would long ago have discovered that heat, and therefore food, is economized by two or three nesting together.

One day in early spring, a chipmunk that lived near me met with a terrible adventure, the memory of which will probably be handed down through many generations of its family. I was sitting in the summer-house with Nig the cat upon my knee, when the chipmunk came out of its den a few feet away, and ran quickly to a pile of chestnut posts about twenty yards from where I sat. Nig saw it, and was off my lap upon the floor in an instant. I spoke sharply to the cat, when she sat down and folded her paws under her, and regarded the squirrel, as I thought, with only a dreamy kind of interest. I fancied she thought it a hopeless case there amid that pile of posts. "That is not your game, Nig," I said, "so spare yourself any anxiety." Just then I was called to the house,

where I was detained about five minutes. As I returned, I met Nig coming to the house with the chipmunk in her mouth. She had the air of one who had won a wager. She carried the chipmunk by the throat, and its body hung limp from her mouth. I quickly took the squirrel from her, and reproved her sharply. It lay in my hand as if dead, though I saw no marks of the cat's teeth upon it. Presently it gasped for its breath, then again and again. I saw that the cat had simply choked it. Quickly the film passed off its eyes, its heart began visibly to beat, and slowly the breathing became regular. I carried it back, and laid it down in the door of its den. In a moment it crawled or kicked itself in. In the afternoon I placed a handful of corn there, to express my sympathy, and as far as possible make amends for Nig's cruel treatment.

Not till four or five days had passed did my little neighbor emerge again from its den, and then only for a moment. That terrible black monster with the large green-yellow eyes,—it might be still lurking near. How the black monster had captured the alert and restless squirrel so quickly, under the circumstances, was a great mystery to me. Was not its eye as sharp as the cat's, and its movements as quick? Yet cats do have the secret of catching squirrels, and birds, and mice, but I have never yet had the luck to see it done.

It was not very long before the chipmunk was going to and from its den as usual, though the dread of the black monster seemed ever before it, and gave speed and extra alertness to all its movements. In early summer four young chipmunks emerged from the den, and ran freely about. There was nothing to disturb them, for, alas! Nig herself was now dead.

One summer day I watched a cat for nearly a half hour trying her arts upon a chipmunk that sat upon a pile of stone. Evidently her game was to stalk him. She had cleared half the distance, or about twelve feet, that separated the chipmunk from a dense Norway spruce, when I chanced to become a spectator of the little drama. There sat the cat crouched low on the grass, her big yellow eyes fixed upon the chipmunk, and there sat the chipmunk at the mouth of his den, motionless, with his eye fixed upon the cat. For a long time neither moved. "Will the cat bind him with her fatal spell?" I thought. Sometimes her head slowly lowered and her eyes seemed to dilate, and I fancied she was about to spring. But she did not. The distance was too great to be successfully cleared in one bound. Then the squirrel moved nervously, but kept his eye upon the enemy. Then the cat evidently grew tired and relaxed a little and looked behind her. Then she crouched again and riveted her gaze upon the squirrel. But the latter would not be hypnotized; it shifted its position a few times and finally quickly entered its den, when the cat soon slunk away.

In digging his hole, it is evident that the chipmunk carries away the loose soil. Never a grain of it is seen in front of his door. Those pockets of his probably stand him in good stead on such occasions. Only in one instance have I seen a pile of earth before the entrance to a chipmunk's den, and that was where the builder had begun his house late in November, and was probably too much hurried to remove this ugly mark from before his door. I used to pass his place every morning in my walk, and my eye always fell upon that little pile of red, freshly dug soil. A little later I used frequently to surprise the squirrel furnishing his house, carrying in dry leaves of the maple and plane tree. He would seize a large leaf and with both hands stuff it into his cheek pockets, and then carry it into his den. I saw him on several different days occupied in this way. I trust he had secured his winter stores, though I am a little doubtful. He was hurriedly making himself a new home, and the cold of December was upon us while he was yet at work. It may be that he had moved the

stores from his old quarters, wherever they were, and again it may be that he had been dispossessed of both his house and provender by some other chipmunk.

When nuts or grain are not to be had, these thrifty little creatures will find some substitute to help them over the winter. Two chipmunks near my study were occupied many days in carrying in cherry pits which they gathered beneath a large cherry-tree that stood ten or twelve rods away. As Nig was no longer about to molest them, they grew very fearless, and used to spin up and down the garden path to and from their source of supplies in a way quite unusual with these timid creatures. After they had got enough cherry pits, they gathered the seed of a sugar maple that stood near. Many of the keys remained upon the tree after the leaves had fallen, and these the squirrels harvested. They would run swiftly out upon the ends of the small branches, reach out for the maple keys, snip off the wings, and deftly slip the nut or samara into their cheek pockets. Day after day in late autumn, I used to see them thus occupied.

As I have said, I have no evidence that more than one chipmunk occupies the same den. One March morning, after a light fall of snow, I saw where one had come up out of his hole, which was in the side of our path to the vineyard, and after a moment's survey of the surroundings had started off on his travels. I followed the track to see where he had gone. He had passed through my woodpile, then under the beehives, then around the study and under some spruces and along the slope to the hole of a friend of his, about sixty yards from his own. Apparently he had gone in here, and then his friend had come forth with him, for there were two tracks leading from his doorway. I followed them to a third humble entrance, not far off, where the tracks were so numerous that I lost the trail. It was pleasing to see the evidence of their morning sociability written there upon the new snow.

One of the enemies of the chipmunk, as I discovered lately, is the weasel. I was sitting in the woods one autumn day when I heard a small cry, and a rustling amid the branches of a tree a few rods beyond me. Looking thither, I saw a chipmunk fall through the air, and catch on a limb twenty of more feet from the ground. He appeared to have dropped from near the top of the tree.

He secured his hold upon the small branch that had luckily intercepted his fall, and sat perfectly still. In a moment more I saw a weasel—one of the smaller red varieties—come down the trunk of the tree, and begin exploring the branches on a level with the chipmunk.

I saw in a moment what had happened. The weasel had driven the squirrel from his retreat in the rocks and stones beneath, and had pressed him so closely that he had taken refuge in the top of a tree. But weasels can climb trees, too, and this one had tracked the frightened chipmunk to the topmost branch, where he had tried to seize him. Then the squirrel had, in horror, let go his hold, screamed, and fallen through the air, till he struck the branch as just described. Now his bloodthirsty enemy was looking for him again, apparently relying entirely upon his sense of smell to guide him to the game.

How did the weasel know the squirrel had not fallen clear to the ground? He certainly did know, for when he reached the same tier of branches, he began exploring them. The chipmunk sat transfixed with fear, frozen with terror, not twelve feet away, and yet the weasel saw him not.

Round and round, up and down, he went on the branches, exploring them over and over. How he hurried, lest the trail get cold! How subtle and cruel and fiendish he looked! His snakelike movements, his tenacity, his speed!

He seemed baffled; he knew his game was near, but he could not strike the spot. The branch, upon the extreme end of which the squirrel sat, ran out and up from the tree seven or eight feet, and then, turning a sharp elbow, swept down and out at right angles with its first course.

The weasel would pause each time at this elbow and turn back. It seemed as if he knew that particular branch held his prey, and yet its crookedness each time threw him out. He would not give it up, but went over his course again and again.

One can fancy the feelings of the chipmunk, sitting there in plain view a few feet away, watching its deadly enemy hunting for the clew. How its little heart must have fairly stood still each time the fatal branch was struck! Probably as a last resort it would again have let go its hold and fallen to the ground, where it might have eluded its enemy awhile longer.

In the course of five or six minutes the weasel gave over the search, and ran hurriedly down the tree to the ground. The chipmunk remained motionless for a long time; then he stirred a little as if hope was reviving. Then he looked nervously about him; then he had recovered himself so far as to change his position. Presently he began to move cautiously along the branch to the bole of the tree; then, after a few moments' delay, he plucked up courage to descend to the ground, where I hope no weasel has disturbed him since.

Riverby

In December 1912 Henry Ford wrote Burroughs a fan letter and offered to send him a car. The machine arrived in January, initiating both friendship and adventure. "Never look back while driving your car!" wrote the seventy-six-year-old Burroughs. "I looked back as I came through the gate, to see if I was going to hit, and the little beast sprang for that tree like a squirrel." The following June, Burroughs visited Ford in Michigan.

There is a mist of green over the woods and splashes of white here and there ... I know a partridge nest with nine eggs. Come and see what some dry leaves cover!

The Life and Letters of John Burroughs

I confess my excursions to the woods are often spoiled, or at least vitiated, by taking my gun and making it a specialty to obtain a bird. I am too much preoccupied and miss everything but the bird. I am not devout and receptive, but eager and inquisitive, and, if I miss the bird, come home dissatisfied.

The full fruition of enjoyment and delight comes when I go out without any purpose except to get nearer the earth and sky, and accept the whole; ready to entertain bird and beast and tree alike—full of faith and self-forgetfulness, and pledged to no special end—all to gain and nothing to lose.

As I saunter through the woods and by the brook, the kindly and hospitable influences of the air and earth come nearer to me; nothing escapes my eye, ear, or nose. A more intimate and harmonious relation is established between me and Nature. I do not outrage the woods; I do not hunt down a bird.

The Heart of Burroughs's Journals

I cannot speak from experience[as to] what it means to belong to a Naturalists Club, since I never belonged to one, but I can see it must have many advantages. It is certainly easier to walk in company than alone, and in the study of nature the multiplied knowledge and enthusiasm of several people ought to be a great advantage; but let me urge you also to cultivate the habit of solitary walks. You will get a little closer to the wild things when alone than in company;—have closer communion with Nature, and absorb more of her spirit. Go with your club on Saturdays, but go alone on Sunday.

The Life and Letters of John Burroughs

It is the slow insensible changes in the equipoise of the elements about us that, in the course of long periods of time, put a new face upon the aspect of the earth. Rapid and noisy changes over large areas, which may have occurred during the geologic ages, we do not now see except in the case of an earthquake. It is the ceaseless activity, both chemical and physical, in the bodies about us, of which we take no note, that transforms the world. Atom by atom the face of the immobile rocks changes.

Under the Apple-Trees

Communing with God is communing with our own hearts, our own best selves, not with something foreign and accidental. Saints and devotees have gone into the wilderness to find God; of course they took God with them, and the silence and detachment enabled them to hear the still, small voice of their own souls, as one hears the ticking of his own watch in the stillness of the night.

The Life and Letters of John Burroughs

You cannot find what the poets find in the woods until you take the poet's heart to the woods. He sees nature through a colored glass, sees it truthfully, but with an indescribable charm added, the aureole of the spirit. A tree, a cloud, a bird, a sunset, have no hidden meaning that the art of the poet is to unlock for us. Every poet shall interpret them differently, and interpret them rightly, because the soul is infinite.

Pepacton

In the fields and woods more than anywhere else all things come to those who wait, because all things are on the move, and are sure sooner or later to come your way.

To absorb a thing is better than to learn it, and we absorb what we enjoy. We learn things at school, we absorb them in the fields and woods and on the farm. When we look upon Nature with fondness and appreciation she meets us halfway and takes a deeper hold upon us than when studiously conned. Hence I say the way of knowledge of Nature is the way of love and enjoyment, and is more surely found in the open air than in the school-room or the laboratory.

Time and Change

How geologic time looks out from the ledges and walls of gray rocks unmindful of us human ephemera that pass! It has seen the mountains decay and the hills grow old. The huge drift boulders rest on the margin of meadows and fields, or stand sentry to the woods, and though races and kingdoms pass, scarcely the change of a wrinkle disturbs their calm stone faces. Yet time gets the better of them also. The frowning ledge melts as inevitably as a snowbank.

Under the Apple-Trees

THE GRIST
OF THE GODS

About all we have in mind when we think of the earth is this thin pellicle of soil with which the granite framework of the globe is clothed—a red and brown film of pulverized and oxidized rock, scarcely thicker, relatively, than the paint or enamel which some women put on their cheeks, and which the rains often wash away as a tear washes off the paint and powder. But it is the main thing to us. Out of it we came and unto it we return. "Earth to earth, and dust to dust." The dust becomes warm and animated for a little while, takes on form and color, stalks about recuperating itself from its parent dust underfoot, and then fades and is resolved into the original earth elements. We are built up out of the ground quite as literally as the trees are, but not quite so immediately. The vegetable is between us and the soil, but our dependence is none the less real. "As common as dust" is one of our sayings, but the common, the universal, is always our mainstay in this world. When we see the dust turned into fruit and flowers and grain by that intangible thing called vegetable life, or into the bodies of men and women by the equally mysterious agency of animal life, we think better of it. The trembling gold of the pond-lily's heart, and its petals like carved snow, are no more a transformation of a little black muck and ooze by the chemistry of the sunbeam than our bodies and minds, too, are a transformation of the soil underfoot.

We are rooted to the air through our lungs and to the soil through our stomachs. We are walking trees and floating plants. The soil which in one form we spurn with our feet, and in another take into our mouths and into our blood—what a composite product it is! It is the grist out of which our bread of life is made, the grist which the mills of the gods, the slow patient gods of Erosion, have been so long grinding—grinding probably more millions of years than we have any idea of. The original stuff, the pulverized granite, was probably not very nourishing, but the fruitful hand of time has made it so. It is the kind of grist that improves with the keeping, and the more the meal-worms have worked in it, the better the bread. Indeed, until it has been eaten and digested by our faithful servitors the vegetables, it does not make the loaf that is our staff of life. The more death has gone into it, the more life comes out of it; the more it is a cemetery, the more it becomes a nursery; the more the rocks perish, the more the fields flourish.

This story of the soil appeals to the imagination. To have a bit of earth to plant, to hoe, to delve in, is a rare privilege. If one stops to consider, one cannot turn it with his spade without emotion. We look back with the mind's eye through the vista of geologic time and we see islands and continents of barren, jagged rocks, not a grain of soil anywhere. We look again and behold a world of rounded hills and fertile valleys and plains, depth of soil where before were frowning rocks. The hand of time with its potent fingers of heat, frost, cloud, and air has passed slowly over the scene, and the miracle is done. The rocks turn to herbage, the fetid gases to the breath of flowers. The mountain melts down into a harvest field; volcanic scoria changes into garden mould; where towered a cliff now basks a green slope; where the strata yawned now bubbles a fountain; where the earth trembled, verdure now undulates. Your lawn and your meadow are built up of the ruins of the foreworld. The leanness of granite and gneiss has become the fat of the land. What transformation and promotion!—the decrepitude of the hills becoming the strength of the plains, the decay of the heights resulting in the renewal of the valleys!

Many of our hills are but the stumps of

mountains which the hand of time has cut down. Hence we may say that if God made the mountains, time made the hills.

What adds to the wonder of the earth's grist is that the millstones that did the work and are still doing it are the gentle forces that career above our heads—the sunbeam, the cloud, the air, the frost. The rain's gentle fall, the air's velvet touch, the sun's noiseless rays, the frost's exquisite crystals, these combined are the agents that crush the rocks and pulverize the mountains, and transform continents of sterile granite into a world of fertile soils. It is as if baby fingers did the work of giant powder and dynamite. Give the clouds and the sunbeams time enough, and the Alps and the Andes disappear before them, or are transformed into plains where corn may grow and cattle graze. The snow falls as softly as down and lies almost as lightly, yet the crags crumble beneath it; compacted by gravity, out of it grew the tremendous ice sheet that ground off the mountain summits, that scooped out lakes and valleys, and modeled our northern landscapes as the sculptor his clay image.

Not only are the mills of the gods grinding here, but the great cosmic mill in the sidereal heavens is grinding also, and some of its dust reaches our planet. Cosmic dust is apparently falling on the earth at all times. It is found in the heart of hailstones and in Alpine snows, and helps make up the mud of the ocean floors.

During the unthinkable time of the revolution of the earth around the sun, the amount of cosmic matter that has fallen upon its surface from out the depths of space must be enormous. It certainly must enter largely into the composition of the soil and of the sedimentary rocks. Celestial dirt we may truly call it, star dust, in which we plant our potatoes and grain and out of which Adam was made, and every son of man since Adam—the divine soil in very fact, the garden of the Eternal, contributed to by the heavens above and all the vital forces below, incorruptible, forever purifying itself, clothing the rocky framework of the globe as with flesh and blood, making the earth truly a mother with a teeming fruitful womb, and her hills veritable mammary glands. The iron in the fruit and vegetables we eat, which thence goes into our blood, may, not very long ago, have formed a part of the cosmic dust that drifted for untold ages along the highways of planets and suns.

The soil underfoot, or that we turn with our plow, how it thrills with life or the potencies of life! What a fresh, good odor it exhales when we turn it with our spade or plow in spring! It is good. No wonder children and horses like to eat it!

How inert and dead it looks, yet what silent, potent fermentations are going on there—millions and trillions of minute organisms ready to further your scheme of agriculture or horticulture. Plant your wheat or your corn in it, and behold the miracle of a birth of a plant or a tree. How it pushes up, fed and stimulated by the soil, through the agency of heat and moisture! It makes visible to the eye the life that is latent or held in suspense there in the cool, impassive ground. The acorn, the chestnut, the maple keys, have but to lie on the surface of the moist earth to feel its power and send down rootlets to meet it.

From one point of view, what a ruin the globe is!—worn and crumbled and effaced beyond recognition, had we known it in its youth. Where once towered mountains are now only their stumps—low, fertile hills or plains. Shake down your great city with its skyscrapers till most of its buildings are heaps of ruins with grass and herbage growing upon them, and you have a hint of what has happened to the earth.

Again, one cannot but reflect what a sucked orange the earth will be in the course of a few more centuries. Our civilization is terribly expensive to all its natural resources; one hundred years of modern life doubtless exhausts its stores more than a millennium of the life of antiquity. Its coal and oil will be about used up, all its mineral wealth greatly depleted, the fertility of its soil will have been washed into the sea through the drainage of its cities, its wild game will be nearly extinct, its primitive forests gone, and soon how nearly bankrupt the planet will be!

There is no better illustration of the way decay and death play into the hands of life than the soil underfoot. The earth dies daily and has done so through countless ages. But life and youth spring forever from its decay; indeed, could not spring at all till the decay began. All the soil was once rock, perhaps many times rock, as the water that flows by may have been many times ice.

The soft, slow, aerial forces, how long and patiently they have worked! Oxygen has played its part in the way of oxidation and dioxidation of minerals. Carbon or carbonic acid has played its part, hydrogen has played its. Even granite yields slowly but surely to the action of rain-water. The sun is of course the great dynamo that runs the earth machinery and, through moisture and the air currents, reduces the rocks to soil. Without solar heat we should have no rain, and without rain we should have no soil. The decay of a mountain makes a hill of fertile fields. The soil, as we know it, is the product of three great processes—mechanical, chemical, and vital—which have been going on for untold ages. The mechanical we see in the friction of winds and waves and the grinding of glaciers, and in the destructive effects of heat and cold upon the rocks; the chemical in the solvent power of rain-water and of water charged with various acids and gases. The soil is rarely the color of the underlying rock from which it came, by reason of the action of the various

gases of the atmosphere. Iron is black, but when turned into rust by the oxygen of the air, it is red.

The vital processes that have contributed to the soil we see going on about us in the decay of animal and vegetable matter. It is this process that gives the humus to the soil, in fact, almost humanizes it, making it tender and full of sentiment and memories, as it were, so that it responds more quickly to our needs and to our culture. The elements of the soil remember all those forms of animal and vegetable life of which they once made a part, and they take them on again the more readily. Hence the quick action of wood ashes upon vegetable life. Iron and lime and phosphorus that have once been taken up by growing plants and trees seem to have acquired new properties, and are the more readily taken up again.

The soil, like mankind, profits by experience, and grows deep and mellow with age. Turn up the cruder subsoil to the sun and air and to vegetable life, and after a time its character is changed; it becomes more gentle and kindly and more fertile.

All things are alike or under the same laws—the rocks, the soil, the soul of man, the trees in the forest, the stars in the sky. We have fertility, depth, geniality, in the ground underfoot, on the same terms upon which we have these things in human life and character.

We hardly realize how life itself has stored up life in the soil, how the organic has wedded and blended with the inorganic in the ground we walk upon. Many if not all of the sedimentary rocks that were laid down in the abysms of the old ocean, out of which our soil has been produced, and that are being laid down now, out of which future soils will be produced, were and are largely of organic origin, the leavings of untold myriads of minute marine animals that lived millions of years ago. Our limestone rocks, thousands of feet thick in places, the decomposition of which furnishes some of our most fertile soils, are mainly of plant and animal origin. The chalk hills of England, so smooth and plump, so domestic and mutton-suggesting, as Huxley says, are the leavings of minute creatures called *Globigerinae,* that lived and died in the ancient seas in the remote past. Other similar creatures, *Radiolaria* and diatoms, have played an equally important part in contributing the foundation of our soils. Diatom earth is found in places in Virginia forty feet thick. The coral insects have also contributed their share to the soil-making rocks. Our marl-beds, our phosphatic and carbonaceous rocks, are all largely of animal origin. So that much of our soil has lived and died many times, and has been charged more and more during the geologic ages or eternities with the potencies of life.

Indeed, Huxley, after examining the discoveries of the *Challenger* expedition, says there are good grounds for the belief "that all the chief known constituents of the crust of the earth may have formed part of living bodies; that they may be the 'ash' of protoplasm."

This implies that life first appeared in the sea, and gave rise to untold myriads of minute organisms, that built themselves shells out of the mineral matter held in solution by the water. As these organisms perished, their shells fell to the bottom and formed the sedimentary rocks. In the course of ages these rocks were lifted up above the sea, and their decay and disintegration under the action of the elements formed our soil—our clays, our marls, our green sand—and out of this soil man himself is built up.

I do not wonder that the Creator found the dust of the earth the right stuff to make Adam of. It was half man already. I can easily believe that his spirit was evoked from the same stuff, that it was latent there, and in due time, under the brooding warmth of the creative energy, awoke to life.

If matter is eternal, as science leads us to believe, and creation and recreation a never-ending process, then the present world, with all its myriad forms of the organic and the inorganic, is only one of the infinite number of forms that matter must have assumed in past aeons. The whole substance of the globe must have gone to the making of other globes such a number of times as no array of figures could express. Every one of the sixty or more primary elements that make up our own bodies and the solid earth beneath us must have played the same part in the drama of life and death, growth and decay, organic and inorganic, that it is playing now, and will continue to play through an unending future.

This gross matter seems ever ready to vanish into the transcendental. When the new physics is done with it, what is there left but spirit, or something akin to it? When the physicist has followed matter through all its transformations, its final disguise seems to be electricity. The solid earth is resolvable into electricity, which comes as near to spirit as anything we can find in the universe.

Our senses are too dull and coarse to apprehend the subtle and incessant play of forces about us—the finer play and emanations of matter that go on all about us and through us. From a lighted candle, or gas-jet, or glowing metal shoot corpuscles or electrons, the basic constituents of matter, of inconceivable smallness—a thousand times smaller than an atom of hydrogen—and at the inconceivable speed of 10,000 to 90,000 miles a second. Think how we are bombarded by these bullets as we sit around the lamp or under the gas-jet at night, and are all unconscious of them! We are immersed in a sea of forces and potentialities of which we hardly dream. Of the scale of temperatures, from absolute zero to the heat of the sun, human life knows only a minute fraction. So of the elemental play of forces about us and over us, terrestrial and celestial—too fine for our apprehension on the one hand, and too large on the other—we know but a fraction.

The quivering and the throbbing of the earth under our feet in changes of temperature, the bendings and oscillations of the crust under the tread of the great atmospheric waves, the vital fermentations and oxidations in the soil—are all beyond the reach of our dull senses. We hear the wind in the treetops, but we do not hear the humming of the sap in the trees. We feel the pull of gravity, but we do not feel the medium through which it works. During the solar storms and disturbances all our magnetic and electrical instruments are agitated, but you and I are all unconscious of the agitation.

There are no doubt vibrations from out the depths of space that might reach our ears as sound were they attuned to the ether as the eye is when it receives a ray of light. We might hear the rush of the planets along their orbits, we might hear the explosions and uprushes in the sun; we might hear the wild whirl and dance of the nebulae, where suns and systems are being formed; we might hear the "wreck of matter and the crush of worlds" that evidently takes place now and then in the abysms of space, because all these things must send through the ether impulses and tremblings that reach our planet. But if we felt or heard or saw or were conscious of all that was going on in the universe, what a state of agitation we should be in! Our scale of apprehension is wisely limited, mainly to things that concern our well-being.

But let not care and humdrum deaden us to the wonders and the mysteries amid which we live, nor to the splendors and the glories. We need not translate ourselves in imagination to some other sphere or state of being to find the marvelous, the divine, the transcendent; we need not postpone our day of wonder and appreciation

to some future time and condition. The true inwardness of this gross visible world, hanging like an apple on the bough of the great cosmic tree, and swelling with all the juices and potencies of life, transcends anything we have dreamed of super-terrestrial abodes. It is because of these things, because of the vitality, spirituality, oneness, and immanence of the universe as revealed by science, its condition of transcending time and space, without youth and without age, neither beginning nor ending, neither material nor spiritual, but forever passing from one into the other, that I was early and deeply impressed by Walt Whitman's lines:—

"There was never any more inception than there is now,
Nor any more youth or age than there is now;
And will never be any more perfection than there is now,
Nor any more heaven or hell than there is now."

And I may add, nor any more creation than there is now, nor any more miracles, or glories, or wonders, or immortality, or judgment days, than there are now. And we shall never be nearer God and spiritual and transcendent things than we are now. The babe in its mother's womb is not nearer its mother than we are to the invisible sustaining and mothering powers of the universe, and to its spiritual entities, every moment of our lives.

The doors and windows of the universe are all open; the screens are all transparent. We are not barred or shut off; there is nothing foreign or unlike; we find our own in the stars as in the ground underfoot; this clod may become a man; yon shooting star may help redden his blood.

Whatever is upon the earth is of the earth; it came out of the divine soil, beamed upon by the fructifying heavens, the soul of man not less than his body.

I never see the spring flowers rising from the mould, or the pond-lilies born of the black ooze, that matter does not become transparent and reveal to me the working of the same celestial powers that fashioned the first man from the common dust.

Man's mind is no more a stranger to the earth than is his body. Is not the clod wise? Is not the chemistry underfoot intelligent? Do not the roots of the trees find their way? Do not the birds know their times and seasons? Are not all things about us filled to overflowing with mind-stuff? The cosmic mind is the earth mind, and the earth mind is man's mind, freed but narrowed, with vision but with erring reason, conscious but troubled, and— shall we say?—human but immortal.

Leaf and Tendril

Burroughs built Slabsides, a rustic, bark-covered cabin, in 1895 in the hills about a mile from Riverby. Here he read, wrote, received countless visitors, and grew celery and lettuce in the rich soil he'd cleared.

THE ART OF SEEING THINGS

I do not purpose to attempt to tell my reader how to see things, but only to talk about the art of seeing things, as one might talk of any other art. One might discourse about the art of poetry, or of painting, or of oratory, without any hope of making one's readers or hearers poets or painters or orators.

The science of anything may be taught or acquired by study; the art of it comes by practice or inspiration. The art of seeing things is not something that may be conveyed in rules and precepts; it is a matter vital in the eye and ear, yea, in the mind and soul, of which these are the organs. I have as little hope of being able to tell the reader how to see things as I would have in trying to tell him how to fall in love or to enjoy his dinner. Either he does or he does not, and that is about all there is of it. Some people seem born with eyes in their heads, and others with buttons or painted marbles, and no amount of science can make the one equal to the other in the art of seeing things. The great mass of mankind are, in this respect, like the rank and file of an army: they fire vaguely in the direction of the enemy, and if they hit, it is more a matter of chance than of accurate aim. But here and there is the keen-eyed observer; he is the sharpshooter; his eye selects and discriminates, his purpose goes to the mark.

Even the successful angler seems born, and not made; he appears to know instinctively the ways of trout. The secret is, no doubt, love of the sport. Love sharpens the eye, the ear, the touch; it quickens the feet, it steadies the hand, it arms against the wet and the cold. What we love to do, that we do well. To know is not all; it is only half. To love is the other half. Wordsworth's poet was contented if he might enjoy the things which others understood. This is generally the attitude of the young and of the poetic nature. The man of science, on the other hand, is contented if he may understand the things that others enjoy: that is his enjoyment. Contemplation and absorption for the one; investigation and classification for the other. We probably all have, in varying degrees, one or the other of these ways of enjoying Nature: either the sympathetic and emotional enjoyment of her which the young and the artistic and the poetic temperament have, or the enjoyment through our knowing faculties afforded by natural science, or, it may be, the two combined, as they certainly were in such a man as Tyndall.

But nothing can take the place of love. Love is the measure of life: only so far as we love do we really live. The variety of our interests, the width of our sympathies, the susceptibilities of our hearts—if these do not measure our lives, what does? As the years go by, we are all of us more or less subject to two dangers, the danger of petrifaction and the danger of putrefaction; either that we shall become hard and callous, crusted over with customs and conventions till no new ray of light or of joy can reach us, or that we shall become lax and disorganized, losing our grip upon the real and vital sources of happiness and power. Now, there is no preservative and antiseptic, nothing that keeps one's heart young, like love, like sympathy, like giving one's self with enthusiasm to some worthy thing or cause.

If I were to name the three most precious resources of life, I should say books, friends, and nature; and the greatest of these, at least the most constant and always at hand, is nature. Nature we have always with us, an inexhaustible storehouse of that which moves the heart, appeals to the mind, and fires the imagination,—health to the body, a stimulus to the intellect, and joy to the soul. To the scientist Nature is a storehouse of facts, laws, processes; to the artist she is a storehouse of pictures; to the poet she is a storehouse of images, fancies, a source of inspiration; to the moralist she is a storehouse of precepts and parables; to all she may be a source of knowledge and joy.

2

There is nothing in which people differ more than in their powers of observation. Some are only half alive to what is going on around them. Others, again, are keenly alive: their intelligence, their powers of recognition, are in full force in eye and ear at all times. They see and hear everything, whether it directly concerns them or not. They never pass unseen a familiar face on the street; they are never oblivious of any interesting feature or sound or object in the earth or sky about them. Their power of attention is always on the alert, not by conscious effort, but by natural habit and disposition. Their perceptive faculties may be said to be always on duty. They turn to the outward world a more highly sensitized mind than other people. The things that pass before them are caught and individualized instantly. If they visit new countries, they see the characteristic features of the people and scenery at once. The impression is never blurred or confused. Their powers of observation suggest the sight and scent of wild animals; only, whereas it is fear that sharpens the one, it is love and curiosity that sharpens the other. The mother turkey with her brood sees the hawk when it is a mere speck against the sky; she is, in her solicitude for her young, thinking of hawks, and is on her guard against them. Fear makes keen her eye. The hunter does not see the hawk till his attention is thus called to it by the turkey, because his interests are not endangered; but he outsees the wild creatures of the plain and mountain,—the elk, the antelope, and the mountain-sheep,—he makes it his business to look for them, and his eyes carry farther than do theirs.

We may see coarsely and vaguely, as most people do, noting only masses and unusual appearances, or we may see finely and discriminatingly, taking in the minute and the specific. In a collection of stuffed birds, the other day, I observed that a wood thrush was mounted as in the act of song, its open beak pointing straight to the zenith. The taxidermist had not seen truly. The thrush sings with its beak but slightly elevated. Who has not seen a red squirrel or a gray squirrel running up and down the trunk of a tree? But probably very few have noticed that the position of the hind feet is the reverse in the one case from what it is in the other. In descending they are extended to the rear, the toe-nails hooking to the bark, checking and controlling the fall. In most pictures the feet are shown well drawn up under the body in both cases.

People who discourse pleasantly and accurately about the birds and flowers and external nature generally are not invariably good observers. In their walks do they see anything they did not come out to see? Is there any spontaneous or unpremeditated seeing? Do they make discoveries? Any bird or creature may be hunted down, any nest discovered, if you lay siege to it; but to find what you are not looking for, to catch the shy winks and gestures on every side, to see all the by-play going on around you, missing no significant note or movement, penetrating every screen with your eye-beams—that is to be an observer; that is to have "an eye practiced like a blind man's touch,"—a touch that can distinguish a white horse from a black,—a detective eye that reads the faintest signs. When Thoreau was at Cape Cod, he noticed that the horses there had a certain muscle in their hips inordinately developed by reason of the insecure footing in the ever-yielding sand. Thoreau's vision at times fitted things closely. During some great fête in Paris, the

Empress Eugénie and Queen Victoria were both present. A reporter noticed that when the royal personages came to sit down, Eugénie looked behind her before doing so, to see that the chair was really there, but Victoria seated herself without the backward glance, knowing there must be a seat ready: there always had been, and there always would be, for her. The correspondent inferred that the incident showed the difference between born royalty and hastily made royalty. I wonder how many persons in that vast assembly made this observation; probably very few. It denoted a gift for seeing things.

If our powers of observation were quick and sure enough, no doubt we should see through most of the tricks of the sleight-of-hand man. He fools us because his hand is more dexterous than our eye. He captures our attention, and then commands us to see only what he wishes us to see.

In the field of natural history, things escape us because the actors are small, and the stage is very large and more or less veiled and obstructed. The movement is quick across a background that tends to conceal rather than expose it. In the printed page the white paper plays quite as important a part as the type and the ink; but the book of nature is on a different plan: the page rarely presents a contrast of black and white, or even black and brown, but only of similar tints, gray upon gray, green upon green, or drab upon brown.

By a close observer I do not mean a minute, cold-blooded specialist,—

"a fingering slave,
One who would peep and botanize
Upon his mother's grave,"—

but a man who looks closely and steadily at nature, and notes the individual features of tree and rock and field, and allows no subtle flavor of the night or day, of the place and the season, to escape him. His senses are so delicate that in his evening walk he feels the warm and the cool streaks in the air, his nose detects the most fugitive odors, his ears the most furtive sounds. As he stands musing in the April twilight, he hears that fine, elusive stir and rustle made by the angle-worms reaching out from their holes for leaves and grasses; he hears the whistling wings of the woodcock as it goes swiftly by him in the dusk; he hears the call of the killdee come down out of the March sky; he hears far above him in the early morning the squeaking cackle of the arriving blackbirds pushing north; he hears the soft, prolonged, lulling call of the little owl in the cedars in the early spring twilight; he hears at night the roar of the distant waterfall, and the rumble of the train miles across the country when the air is "hollow;" before a storm he notes how distant objects stand out and are brought near on those brilliant days that we call "weather-breeders." When the mercury is at zero or lower, he notes how the passing trains hiss and simmer as if the rails or wheels were red-hot. He reads the subtle signs of the weather. The stars at night forecast the coming day to him; the clouds at evening and at morning are a sign. He knows there is the wet-weather diathesis and the dry-weather diathesis, or, as Goethe said, water affirmative and water negative, and he interprets the symptoms accordingly. He is keenly alive to all outward impressions. when he descends from the hill in the autumn twilight, he notes the cooler air of the valley like a lake about him; he notes how, at other seasons, the cooler air at times settles down between the mountains like a vast body of water, as shown by the level line of the fog or the frost upon the trees.

The modern man looks at nature with an eye of sympathy and love where the earlier man looked with an eye of fear and superstition. Hence he sees more closely and accurately; science has made his eye steady and clear. To a hasty traveler through the land, the farms and country homes all seem much alike, but to the people born and reared there, what a difference! They have read the fine print that escapes the hurried eye and that is so full of meaning. Every horizon line, every curve in hill or valley, every tree and rock and spring run, every turn in the road and vista in the landscape, has its special features and makes its own impression.

Scott wrote in his journal: "Nothing is so tiresome as walking through some beautiful scene with a minute philosopher, a botanist, or a pebble-gatherer, who is eternally calling your attention from the grand features of the natural picture to look at grasses and chuckie-stanes." No doubt Scott's large, generous way of looking at things kindles the imagination and touches the sentiments more than does this minute way of the specialist. The nature that Scott gives us is like the air and the water that all may absorb, while what the specialist gives us is more like some particular element or substance that only the few can appropriate. But Scott had his specialties, too, the specialties of the sportsman: he was the first to see the hare's eyes as she sat in her form, and he knew the ways of grouse and pheasants and trout. The ideal observer turns the enthusiasm of the sportsman into the channels of natural history, and brings home a finer game than ever fell to shot or bullet. He too has an eye for the fox and the rabbit and the migrating water-fowl, but he sees them with loving and not with murderous eyes.

3

So far as seeing things is an art, it is the art of keeping your eyes and ears open. The art of nature is all in the direction of concealment. The birds, the animals, all the wild creatures, for the most part try to elude your observation. The art of the bird is to hide her nest; the art of the game you are in quest of is to make itself invisible. The flower seeks to attract the bee and the moth by its color and perfume, because they are of service to it; but I presume it would hide from the excursionists and the picnickers if it could, because they extirpate it. Power of attention and a mind sensitive to outward objects, in these lies the secret of seeing things. Can you bring all your faculties to the front, like a house with many faces at the doors and windows; or do you live retired within yourself, shut up in your own meditations? The thinker puts all the powers of his mind in reflection: the observer puts all the powers of his mind in perception; every faculty is directed outward; the whole mind sees through the eye and hears through the ear. He has an objective turn of mind as opposed to a subjective. A person with the latter turn of mind sees little. If you are occupied with your own thoughts, you may go through a museum of curiosities and observe nothing.

Of course one's powers of observation may be cultivated as well as anything else. The senses of seeing and hearing may be quickened and trained as well as the sense of touch. Blind persons come to be marvelously acute in their powers of touch. Their feet find the path and keep it. They come to know the lay of the land through this sense, and recognize the roads and surfaces they have once traveled over. Helen Keller reads your speech by putting her hand upon your lips, and is thrilled by the music of an instrument through the same sense of touch. The perceptions of school-children should be trained as well as their powers of reflection and memory. A teacher in Connecticut, Miss Aiken,—whose work on mind-training I commend to all teachers,—has hit upon a simple and ingenious method of doing this. She has a revolving blackboard upon which she writes various figures, numbers, words, sentences, which she exposes to the view of the class for one or two or three seconds, as the case may be, and then asks them to copy or repeat what was written. In time they become astonishingly quick, especially the girls, and can take in a multitude of things at a glance. Detectives, I am told, are trained after a similar method; a man is led quickly by a show-window, for instance, and asked to name and describe the objects he saw there. Life itself is of course more or less a school of this kind, but the power of concentrated attention in most persons needs stimulating. Here comes in the benefit of manual-training schools. To *do* a thing, to make something, the powers of the mind must be focused. A boy in building a boat will get something that all the books in the world cannot give him. The concrete, the definite, the discipline of real things, the educational values that lie here, are not enough appreciated.

4

The book of nature is like a page written over or printed upon with different-sized characters and in many different languages, interlined and cross-lined, and with a great variety of marginal notes and references. There is coarse print and fine print; there are obscure signs and hieroglyphics. We all read the large type more or less appreciatively, but only the students and lovers of nature read the fine lines and the footnotes. It is a book which he reads best who goes most slowly or even tarries long by the way. He who runs may read some things. We may take in the general features of sky, plain, and river from the express train, but only the pedestrian, the saunterer, with eyes in his head and love in his heart, turns every leaf and peruses every line. One man sees only the migrating water-fowls and the larger birds of the air; another sees the passing kinglets and hurrying warblers as well. For my part, my delight is to linger long over each page of this marvelous record, and to dwell fondly upon its most obscure text.

I take pleasure in noting the minute things about me. I am interested even in the ways of the wild bees, and in all the little dramas and tragedies that occur in field and wood. One June day, in my walk, as I crossed a rather dry, high-lying field, my attention was attracted by small mounds of fresh earth all over the ground, scarcely more than a handful in each. On looking closely, I saw that in the middle of each mound there was a hole not quite so large as a lead-pencil. Now, I had never observed these mounds before, and my curiosity was aroused. "Here is some fine print," I said, "that I have overlooked." So I set to work to try to read it; I waited for a sign of life. Presently I saw here and there a bee hovering about over the mounds. It looked like the honey-bee, only less pronounced in color and manner. One of them alighted on one of the mounds near me, and was about to disappear in the hole in the centre when I caught it in my hand. Though it stung me, I retained it and looked it over and in the process was stung several times; but the pain was slight. I saw it was one of our native wild bees, cousin to the leaf-rollers, that build their nests under stones and in decayed fence-rails. (In Packard I found it described under the name of *Andrena*.) Then I inserted a small weed-stalk into one of the holes, and, with a little trowel I carried, proceeded to dig out the nest. The hole was about a foot deep; at the bottom of it I found a little semi-transparent, membranous sac or cell, a little larger than that of the honey-bee; in this sac was a little pellet of yellow pollen—a loaf of bread for the young grub when the egg should have hatched. I explored other nests and found them all the same. This discovery was not a great addition to my sum of natural knowledge, but it was something. Now when I see the signs in a field, I know what they mean; they indicate the tiny earthen cradles of *Andrena*.

Near by I chanced to spy a large hole in the turf, with no mound of soil about it. I could put the end of my little finger into it. I peered down, and saw the gleam of two small, bead-like eyes. I knew it to be the den of the wolf-spider. Was she waiting for some blundering insect to tumble in? I say she, because the real ogre among the spiders is the female. The male is small and of little consequence. A few days later I paused by this den again and saw the members of the ogress scattered about her own door. Had some insect Jack the Giant-Killer been there, or had a still more formidable ogress, the sand-hornet, dragged her forth and carried away her limbless body to her den in the bank?

What the wolf-spider does with the earth it excavates in making its den is a mystery. There is no sign of it anywhere about. Does it force its way down by pushing the soil to one side and packing it there firmly? The entrance to the hole usually has a slight rim or hem to keep the edge from crumbling in.

As it happened, I chanced upon another interesting footnote that very day. I was on my way to a muck swamp in the woods, to see if the showy lady's-slipper was in bloom. Just on the margin of the swamp, in the deep shade of the hemlocks, my eye took note of some small, unshapely creature crawling hurriedly over the ground. I stooped down, and saw it was some large species of moth just out of its case, and in a great hurry to find a suitable place in which to hang itself up and give its wings a chance to unfold before the air dried them. I thrust a small twig in its way, which it instantly seized upon. I lifted it gently, carried it to drier ground, and fixed the stick in the fork of a tree, so that the moth hung free a few feet from the ground. Its body was distended nearly to the size of one's little finger, and surmounted by wings that were so crumpled and stubby that they seemed quite rudimentary. The creature evidently knew what it wanted, and knew the importance of haste. Instantly these rude,

stubby wings began to grow. It was a slow process, but one could see the change from minute to minute. As the wings expanded, the body contracted. By some kind of pumping arrangement air was being forced from a reservoir in the one into the tubes of the other. The wings were not really growing, as they at first seemed to be, but they were unfolding and expanding under this pneumatic pressure from the body. In the course of about half an hour the process was completed, and the winged creature hung there in all its full-fledged beauty. Its color was checked black and white like a loon's back, but its name I know not. My chief interest in it, aside from the interest we feel in any new form of life, arose from the creature's extreme anxiety to reach a perch where it could unfold its wings. A little delay would doubtless have been fatal to it. I wonder how many human geniuses are hatched whose wings are blighted by some accident or untoward circumstance. Or do the wings of genius always unfold, no matter what the environment may be?

One seldom takes a walk without encountering some of this fine print on nature's page. Now it is a little yellowish-white moth that spreads itself upon the middle of a leaf as if to imitate the droppings of birds; or it is the young cicadas working up out of the ground, and in the damp, cool places building little chimneys or tubes above the surface to get more warmth and hasten their development; or it is a wood-newt gorging a tree-cricket, or a small snake gorging the newt, or a bird song with some striking peculiarity—a strange defect, or a rare excellence. Now it is a shrike impaling his victim, or blue jays mocking and teasing a hawk and dropping quickly into the branches to avoid his angry blows, or a robin hustling a cuckoo out of the tree where her nest is, or a vireo driving away a cowbird, or the partridge blustering about your feet till her young are hidden. One October morning I was walking along the road on the edge of the woods, when I came into a gentle shower of butternuts; one of them struck my hat-brim. I paused and looked about me; here one fell, there another, yonder a third. There was no wind blowing, and I wondered what was loosening the butternuts. Turning my attention to the top of the tree, I soon saw the explanation: a red squirrel was at work gathering his harvest. He would seize a nut, give it a twist, when down it would come; then he would dart to another and another. Farther along I found where he had covered the ground with chestnut burs; he could not wait for the frost and the winds; did he know that the burs would dry and open upon the ground, and that the bitter covering of the butternuts would soon fall away from the nut?

There are three things that perhaps happen near me each season that I have never yet seen—the toad casting its skin, the snake swallowing its young, and the larvae of the moth and butterfly constructing their shrouds. It is a mooted question whether or not the snake does swallow its young, but if there is no other good reason for it, may they not retreat into their mother's stomach to feed? How else are they to be nourished? That the moth larva can weave its own cocoon and attach it to a twig seems more incredible. Yesterday, in my walk, I found a firm, silver-gray cocoon, about two inches long and shaped like an Egyptian mummy (probably *Promethea*), suspended from a branch of a bush by a narrow, stout ribbon twice as long as itself. The fastening was woven around the limb, upon which it turned as if it grew there. I would have given something to have seen the creature perform this feat, and then incase itself so snugly in the silken shroud at the end of this tether. By swinging free, its firm, compact case was in no danger from woodpeckers, as it might have been if resting directly upon a branch or tree-trunk. Near by was the cocoon of another species (*Cecropia*) that was fastened directly to the limb;

but this was vague, loose, and much more involved and net-like. I have seen the downy woodpecker assaulting one of these cocoons, but its yielding surface and webby interior seemed to puzzle and baffle him.

I am interested even in the way each climbing plant or vine goes up the pole, whether from right to left, or from left to right,—that is, with the hands of a clock or against them,—whether it is under the law of the great cyclonic storms of the northern hemisphere, which all move against the hands of a clock, or in the contrary direction, like the cyclones in the southern hemisphere. I take pleasure in noting every little dancing whirlwind of a summer day that catches up the dust or the leaves before me, and every little funnel-shaped whirlpool in the swollen stream or river, whether or not they spin from right to left or the reverse. If I were in the southern hemisphere, I am sure I should note whether these things were under the law of its cyclones in this respect or under the law of ours. As a rule, our twining plants and toy whirlwinds copy our revolving storms and go against the hands of the clock. But there are exceptions. While the bean, the bittersweet, the morning-glory, and others go up from left to right, the hop, the wild buckwheat, and some others go up from right to left. Most of our forest trees show a tendency to wind one way or the other, the hard woods going in one direction, and the hemlocks and pines and cedars and butternuts and chestnuts in another. In different localities, or on different geological formations, I find these directions reversed. I recall one instance in the case of a hemlock six or seven inches in diameter, where this tendency to twist had come out of the grain, as it were, and shaped the outward form of the tree, causing it to make, in an ascent of about thirty feet, one complete revolution about a larger tree close to which it grew. On a smaller scale I have seen the same thing in a pine.

Persons lost in the woods or on the plains, or traveling at night, tend, I believe, toward the left. The movements of men and women, it is said, differ in this respect, one sex turning to the right and the other to the left.

I had lived in the world more than fifty years before I noticed a peculiarity about the rays of light one often sees diverging from an opening, or a series of openings, in the clouds, namely, that they are like spokes in a wheel, the hub, or centre, of which appears to be just there in the vapory masses, instead of being, as is really the case, nearly ninety-three millions of miles beyond. The beams of light that come through cracks or chinks in a wall do not converge in this way, but to the eye run parallel to one another. There is another fact: this fan-shaped display of converging rays is always immediately in front of the observer; that is, exactly between him and the sun, so that the central spoke or shaft in his front is always perpendicular. You cannot see this fan to the right or left of the sun, but only between you and it. Hence, as in the case of the rainbow, no two persons see exactly the same rays.

The eye sees what it has the means of seeing, and its means of seeing are in proportion to the love and desire behind it. The eye is informed and sharpened by the thought. My boy sees ducks on the river where and when I cannot, because at certain seasons he thinks ducks and dreams ducks. One season my neighbor asked me if the bees had injured my grapes. I said, "No; the bees never injure my grapes."

"They do mine," he replied; "they puncture the skin for the juice, and at times the clusters are covered with them."

"No," I said, "it is not the bees that puncture the skin; it is the birds."

"What birds?"

"The orioles."

"But I haven't seen any orioles," he rejoined.

"We have," I continued, "because at this season we think orioles; we have learned by experience how destructive these birds are in the vineyard, and we are on the lookout for them; our eyes and ears are ready for them."

If we think birds, we shall see birds wherever we go; if we think arrowheads, as Thoreau did, we shall pick up arrowheads in every field. Some people have an eye for four-leaved clovers; they see them as they walk hastily over the turf, for they already have them in their eyes. I once took a walk with the late Professor Eaton of Yale. He was just then specially interested in the mosses, and he found them, all kinds, everywhere. I can see him yet, every few minutes upon his knees, adjusting his eye-glasses before some rare specimen. The beauty he found in them, and pointed out to me, kindled my enthusiasm also. I once spent a summer day at the mountain home of a well-known literary woman and editor. She lamented the absence of birds about her house. I named a half-dozen or more I had heard or seen in her trees within an hour—the indigo-bird, the purple finch, the yellowbird, the veery thrush, the red-eyed vireo, the song sparrow.

"Do you mean to say you have seen or heard all these birds while sitting here on my porch?" she inquired.

"I really have," I said.

"I do not see them or hear them," she replied, "and yet I want to very much."

"No," said I; "you only *want to want* to see and hear them."

You must have the bird in your heart before you can find it in the bush.

I was sitting in front of a farmhouse one day in company with the local Nimrod. In a maple tree in front of us I saw the great crested flycatcher. I called the hunter's attention to it, and asked him if he had ever seen that bird before. No, he had not; it was a new bird to him. But he probably had seen it scores of times,—seen it without regarding it. It was not the game he was in quest of, and his eye heeded it not.

Human and artificial sounds and objects thrust themselves upon us; they are within our sphere, so to speak: but the life of nature we must meet halfway; it is shy, withdrawn, and blends itself with a vast neutral background. We must be initiated; it is an order the secrets of which are well guarded.

Leaf and Tendril

The writings of Emerson and Thoreau drew readers to seek them personally. My books do not bring readers to me, but send them to Nature. I take credit to myself on this account.

The Heart of Burroughs's Journals

The river idealizes the landscape. It multiplies and heightens the beauty of the day and season. A fair day it makes more fair, and a wild, tempestuous day it makes more wild. The face of winter it makes doubly rigid and corpse-like, and to the face of spring it adds new youth and sparkle.

The Heart of Burroughs's Journals

The beauty of nature includes all that is called beautiful, as its flower; and all that is not called beautiful, as its stock and roots.

Indeed, when I go to the woods or the fields, or ascend to the hilltop, I do not seem to be gazing upon beauty at all, but to be breathing it like the air. I am not dazzled or astonished; I am in no hurry to look lest it be gone. I would not have the litter and debris removed, or the banks trimmed, or the ground painted. What I enjoy is commensurate with the earth and sky itself. It clings to the rocks and trees; it is kindred to the roughness and savagery; it rises from every tangle and chasm; it perches on the dry oak-stubs with the hawks and buzzards; the crows shed it from their wings and weave it into their nests of coarse sticks; the fox barks it, the cattle low it, and every mountain path leads to its haunts. I am not a spectator of, but a participator in it. It is not an adornment; its roots strike to the centre of the earth.

Birds and Poets

You are eligible to any good fortune when you are in the condition to enjoy a walk. When the air and the water taste sweet to you, how much else will taste sweet! When the exercise of your limbs affords you pleasure, and the play of your senses upon the various objects and shows of nature quickens and stimulates your spirit, your relation to the world and to yourself is what it should be,—simple and direct and wholesome.

Pepacton

Now is the time of the illuminated woods, they have a sense of sunshine, even on a cloudy day, given by the yellow foliage; every leaf glows like a tiny lamp; one walks through their lighted halls with curious enjoyment.

The Heart of Burroughs's Journals

How beautifully the leaves grow old! How full of light and color are their last days! There are exceptions, of course. The leaves of most of the fruit trees fade and wither and fall ingloriously. They bequeath their heritage of color to their fruit. Upon it they lavish hues which other trees lavish upon their leaves . . . .

But in October what a feast to the eye our woods and groves present! The whole body of the air seems enriched by their calm, slow radiance. They are giving back the light they have been absorbing from the sun all summer.

Under the Maples

We cannot all find the same things in Nature. She is all things to all men .... In her are "all manners of tastes," science, art, poetry, utility, and good in all. The botanist has one pleasure in her, the ornithologist another, the explorer another, the walker another, and the sportsman another; what all may have is the refreshment and the exhilaration which come from a loving and intelligent scrutiny of her manifold works.

Riverby

The course of the seasons never does run smooth, owing to the unequal distribution of land and water, mountain, wood, and plain.

An equilibrium, however, is usually reached in our climate in October, sometimes the most marked in November, forming the delicious Indian summer; a truce is declared, and both forces, heat and cold, meet and mingle in friendly converse on the field. In the earlier season, this poise of the temperature, this slack-water in nature, comes in May and June; but the October calm is most marked. Day after day, and sometimes week after week, you cannot tell which way the current is setting. Indeed, there is no current, but the season seems to drift a little this way or a little that, just as the breeze happens to freshen a little in one quarter or the other.

Winter Sunshine

THE GOSPEL OF NATURE

The other day a clergyman who described himself as a preacher of the gospel of Christ wrote, asking me to come and talk to his people on the gospel of Nature. The request set me to thinking whether or not Nature has any gospel in the sense the clergyman had in mind, any message that is likely to be specially comforting to the average orthodox religious person. I suppose the parson wished me to tell his flock what I had found in Nature that was a strength or a solace to myself.

What had all my many years of journeyings to Nature yielded me that would supplement or reinforce the gospel he was preaching? Had the birds taught me any valuable lessons? Had the four-footed beasts? Had the insects? Had the flowers, the trees, the soil, the coming and the going of the seasons? Had I really found sermons in stones, books in running brooks and good in everything? Had the lilies of the field, that neither toil nor spin, and yet are more royally clad than Solomon in all his glory, helped me in any way to clothe myself with humility, with justice, with truthfulness?

It is not easy for one to say just what he owes to all these things. Natural influences work indirectly as well as directly; they work upon the subconscious, as well as upon the conscious, self. That I am a saner, healthier, more contented man, with truer standards of life, for all my loiterings in the fields and woods, I am fully convinced.

That I am less social, less interested in my neighbors and in the body politic, more inclined to shirk civic and social responsibilities and to stop my ears against the brawling of the reformers, is perhaps equally true.

One thing is certain, in a hygienic way I owe much to my excursions to Nature. They have helped to clothe me with health, if not with humility; they have helped sharpen and attune all my senses; they have kept my eyes in such good trim that they have not failed me for one moment during all the seventy-five years I have had them; they have made my sense of smell so keen that I have much pleasure in the wild, open-air perfumes, especially in the spring—the delicate breath of the blooming elms and maples and willows, the breath of the woods, of the pastures, of the shore. This keen, healthy sense of smell has made me abhor tobacco and flee from close rooms, and put the stench of cities behind me. I fancy that this whole world of wild, natural perfumes is lost to the tobacco-user and to the city-dweller. Senses trained in the open air are in tune with open-air objects; they are quick, delicate, and discriminating. When I go to town, my ear suffers as well as my nose: the impact of the city upon my senses is hard and dissonant; the ear is stunned, the nose is outraged, and the eye is confused. When I come back, I go to Nature to be soothed and healed, and to have my senses put in tune once more. I know that, as a rule, country or farming folk are not remarkable for the delicacy of their senses, but this is owing mainly to the benumbing and brutalizing effect of continued hard labor. It is their minds more than their bodies that suffer.

When I have dwelt in cities the country was always near by, and I used to get a bite of country soil at least once a week to keep my system normal.

Emerson says that "the day does not seem wholly profane in which we have given heed to some natural object." If Emerson had stopped to qualify his remark, he would have added, if we give heed to it in the right spirit, if we give heed to it as a nature-lover and truth-seeker. Nature love as Emerson knew it, and as Wordsworth knew it, and as any of the choicer spirits of our time have known it, has distinctly a religious value. It does not come to a man or a woman who is wholly absorbed in selfish or worldly or material ends. Except ye become in a measure as little children, ye cannot enter the kingdom of Nature—as Audubon entered it, as Thoreau entered it, as Bryant and Amiel entered it, and as all those enter it who make it a resource in their lives and an instrument of their culture. The forms and creeds of religion change, but the sentiment of religion—the wonder and reverence and love we feel in the presence of the inscrutable universe—persists. Indeed, these seem to be renewing their life to-day in this growing love for all natural objects and in this increasing tenderness toward all forms of life. If we do not go to church so much as did our fathers, we go to the woods much more, and are much more inclined to make a temple of them than they were.

We now use the word Nature very much as our fathers used the word God, and, I suppose, back of it all we mean the power that is everywhere present and active, and in whose lap the visible universe is held and nourished. It is a power that we can see and touch and hear, and realize every moment of our lives how absolutely we are dependent upon it. There are no atheists or skeptics in regard to this power. All men see how literally we are its children, and all men learn how swift and sure is the penalty of disobedience to its commands.

Our associations with Nature vulgarize it and rob it of its divinity. When we come to see that the celestial and the terrestrial are one, that time and eternity are one, that mind and matter are one, that death and life are one, that there is and can be nothing not inherent in Nature, then we no longer look for or expect a far-off, unknown God.

Nature teaches more than she preaches. There are no sermons in stones. It is easier to get a spark out of a stone than a moral.

Even when it contains a fossil, it teaches history rather than morals. It comes down from the foreworld an undigested bit that has resisted the tooth and maw of time, and can tell you many things if you have the eye to read them. The soil upon which it lies or in which it is imbedded was rock, too, back in geologic time, but the mill that ground it up passed the fragment of stone through without entirely reducing it. Very likely it is made up of the minute remains of innumerable tiny creatures that lived and died in the ancient seas. Very likely it was torn from its parent rock and brought to the place where it now lies by the great ice-flood that many tens of thousands of years ago crept slowly but irresistibly down out of the North over the greater part of all the northern continents.

But all this appeals to the intellect, and contains no lesson for the moral nature. If we are to find sermons in stones, we are to look for them in the relations of the stones to other things—when they are out of place, when they press down the grass or the flowers, or impede the plow, or dull the scythe, or usurp the soil, or shelter vermin, as do old institutions and old usages that have had their day. A stone that is much knocked about gets its sharp angles worn off, as do men. "A rolling stone gathers no moss," which is not bad for the stone, as moss hastens decay. "Killing two birds with one stone" is a bad saying, because it reminds boys to stone the birds, which is bad for both boys and birds. But "People who live in glass houses should not throw stones" is on the right side of the account, as it discourages stone-throwing and reminds us that we are no better than our neighbors.

The lesson in running brooks is that motion is a great purifier and health-producer. When the brook ceases to run, it soon stagnates. It keeps in touch with the great vital currents when it is in motion, and unites with other brooks to help make the river. In motion it soon leaves all mud and sediment behind. Do not proper work and the exercise of will power have the same effect upon our lives?

The other day in my walk I came upon a sap-bucket that had been left standing by the maple tree all the spring and summer. What a bucketful of corruption was that, a mixture of sap and rainwater that had rotted, and smelled to heaven. Mice and birds and insects had been drowned in it, and added to its unsavory character. It was a bit of Nature cut off from the vitalizing and purifying chemistry of the whole. With what satisfaction I emptied it upon the ground while I held my nose and saw it filter into the turf, where I knew it was dying to go and where I knew every particle of the reeking, fetid fluid would soon be made sweet and wholesome again by the chemistry of the soil!

2

I am not always in sympathy with nature-study as pursued in the schools, as if this kingdom could be carried by assault. Such study is too cold, too special, too mechanical; it is likely to rub the bloom off Nature. It lacks soul and emotion; it misses the accessories of the open air and its exhilarations, the sky, the clouds, the landscape, and the currents of life that pulse everywhere.

I myself have never made a dead set at studying Nature with note-book and field-glass in hand. I have rather visited with her. We have walked together or sat down together, and our intimacy grows with the seasons. What I have learned about her ways I have learned easily, almost unconsciously, while fishing or camping or idling about. My desultory habits have their disadvantages, no doubt, but they have their advantages also. A too strenuous pursuit defeats itself. In the fields and woods more than anywhere else all things come to those who wait, because all things are on the move, and are sure sooner or later to come your way.

To absorb a thing is better than to learn it, and we absorb what we enjoy. We learn things at school, we absorb them in the fields and woods and on the farm. When we look upon Nature with fondness and appreciation she meets us halfway and takes a deeper hold upon us than when studiously conned. Hence I say the way of knowledge of Nature is the way of love and enjoyment, and is more surely found in the open air than in the school-room or the laboratory. The other day I saw a lot of college girls dissecting cats and making diagrams of the circulation and muscle-attachments, and I thought it pretty poor business unless the girls were taking a course in comparative anatomy with a view to some occupation in life. What is the moral and intellectual value of this kind of knowledge to those girls? Biology is, no doubt, a great science in the hands of great men, but it is not for all. I myself have got along very well without it. I am sure I can learn more of what I want to know from a kitten on my knee than from the carcass of a cat in the laboratory. Darwin spent eight years dissecting barnacles; but he was Darwin, and did not stop at barnacles, as these college girls are pretty sure to stop at cats. He dissected and put together again in his mental laboratory the whole system of animal life, and the upshot of his work was a tremendous gain to our understanding of the universe.

I would rather see the girls in the fields and woods studying and enjoying living nature, training their eyes to see correctly and their hearts to respond intelligently. What is knowledge without enjoyment, without love? It is sympathy, appreciation, emotional experience, which refine and elevate and breathe into exact knowledge the breath of life. My own interest is in living nature as it moves and flourishes about me winter and summer.

I know it is one thing to go forth as a nature-lover, and quite another to go forth in a spirit of cold, calculating, exact science. I call my-self a nature-lover and not a scientific naturalist. All that science has to tell me is welcome, is, in-deed, eagerly sought for. I must know as well as feel. I am not merely contented, like Wordsworth's poet, to enjoy what others understand. I must understand also; but above all things I must enjoy. How much of my enjoyment springs from my knowledge I do not know. The joy of knowing is very great; the delight of picking up the threads of

Dating back to his days as a country schoolmaster, Burroughs enjoyed the company of children. Once he gave a "lockjaw party" for a group of visiting youngsters—cooking maple syrup to a waxy consistency and cooling the chewy treat in a pan of snow.

meaning here and there, and following them through the maze of confusing facts, I know well. When I hear the woodpecker drumming on a dry limb in spring or the grouse drumming in the woods, and know what it is all for, why, that knowledge, I suppose, is part of my enjoyment. The other part is the associations that those sounds call up as voicing the arrival of spring: they are the drums that lead the joyous procession.

To enjoy understandingly, that, I fancy, is the great thing to be desired. When I see the large ichneumon-fly, *Thalessa,* making a loop over her back with her long ovipositor and drilling a hole in the trunk of a tree, I do not fully appreciate the spectacle till I know she is feeling for the burrow of a tree-borer, *Tremex,* upon the larvae of which her own young feed. She must survey her territory like an oil-digger and calculate where she is likely to strike oil, which in her case is the burrow of her host *Tremex.* There is a vast series of facts in natural history like this that are of little interest until we understand them. They are like the outside of a book which may attract us, but which can mean little to us until we have opened and perused its pages.

The nature-lover is not looking for mere facts, but for meanings, for something he can translate into the terms of his own life. He wants facts, but significant facts—luminous facts that throw light upon the ways of animate and inanimate nature. A bird picking up crumbs from my window-sill does not mean much to me. It is a pleasing sight and touches a tender cord, but it does not add much to my knowledge of bird-life. But when I see a bird pecking and fluttering angrily at my window-pane, as I now and then do in spring, apparently under violent pressure to get in, I am witnessing a significant comedy in bird-life, one that illustrates the limits of animal instinct. The bird takes its own reflected image in the glass for a hated rival, and is bent on demolishing it. Let the assaulting bird get a glimpse of the inside of the empty room through a broken pane, and it is none the wiser; it returns to the assault as vigorously as ever.

The fossils in the rocks did not mean much to the earlier geologists. They looked upon them as freaks of Nature, whims of the creative energy, or vestiges of Noah's flood. You see they were blinded by the preconceived notions of the six-day theory of creation.

3

I do not know that the bird has taught me any valuable lesson. Indeed, I do not go to Nature to be taught. I go for enjoyment and companionship. I go to bathe in her as in a sea; I go to give my eyes and ears and all my senses a free, clean field and to tone up my spirits by her "primal sanities." If the bird has not preached to me, it has added to the resources of my life, it has widened the field of my interests, it has afforded me another beautiful object to love, and has helped make me feel more at home in this world. To take the birds out of my life would be like lopping off so many branches from the tree: there is so much less surface of leafage to absorb the sunlight and bring my spirits in contact with the vital currents. We cannot pursue any natural study with love and enthusiasm without the object of it becoming a part of our lives. The birds, the flowers, the trees, the rocks, all become linked with our lives and hold the key to our thoughts and emotions.

Not till the bird becomes a part of your life can its coming and its going mean much to you. And it becomes a part of your life when you have taken heed of it with interest and affection, when you have established associations with it, when it voices the spring or the summer to you, when it calls up the spirit of the woods or the fields or the shore. When year after year you have heard the veery in the beech and birch woods along the trout streams, or the wood thrush May after May in the groves where you have walked or sat, and the bobolink summer after summer in the home meadows, or the vesper sparrow in the upland pastures where you have loitered as a boy or mused as a man, these birds will really be woven into the texture of your life.

What lessons the birds have taught me I cannot recall; what a joy they have been to me I know well. In a new place, amid strange scenes, theirs are the voices and the faces of old friends. In Bermuda the bluebirds and the catbirds and the cardinals seemed to make American territory of it. Our birds had annexed the island despite the Britishers.

For many years I have in late April seen the redpoll warbler, perhaps for only a single day, flitting about as I walked or worked. It is usually my first warbler, and my associations with it are very pleasing. But I really did not know how pleasing until, one March day, when I was convalescing from a serious illness in one of our seacoast towns, I chanced to spy the little traveler in a vacant lot along the street, now upon the ground, now upon a bush, nervous and hurried as usual, uttering its sharp chip, and showing the white in its tail. The sight gave me a real home feeling. It did me more good than the medicine I was taking. It instantly made a living link with many past springs. Anything that calls up a happy past, how it warms the present! There, too, that same day I saw my first meadowlark of the season in a vacant lot, flashing out the white quills in her tail, and walking over the turf in the old, erect, alert manner. The sight was as good as a letter from home, and better: it had a flavor of the wild and of my boyhood days on the old farm that no letter could ever have.

The spring birds always awaken a thrill wherever I am. The first bobolink I hear flying over northward and bursting out in song now and then, full of anticipation of those broad meadows where he will soon be with his mate; or the first swallow twittering joyously overhead, borne on a warm southern breeze; or the first high-hole sounding out his long, iterated call from the orchard or field —how all these things send a wave of emotion over me!

Pleasures of another kind are to find a new bird, and to see an old bird in a new place, as I did recently in the old sugar-bush where I used to help gather and boil sap as a boy. It was the log-cock, or pileated woodpecker, a rare bird anywhere, and one I had never seen before on the old farm. I heard his loud cackle in a maple tree, saw him flit from branch to branch for a few moments, and then launch out and fly toward a distant wood. But he left an impression with me that I should be sorry to have missed.

Nature stimulates our aesthetic and our intellectual life and to a certain extent our religious emotions, but I fear we cannot find much support for our ethical system in the ways of wild Nature. I know our artist naturalist, Ernest Thompson Seton, claims to find what we may call the biological value of the Ten Commandments in the lives of the wild animals; but I cannot make his reasoning hold water, at least not much of it. Of course the Ten Commandments are not arbitrary laws. They are largely founded upon the needs of the social organism; but whether they have the same foundation in the needs of animal life apart from man, apart from the world of moral obligation, is another question. The animals are neither moral nor immoral: they are unmoral; their needs are all physical. It is true that the command against murder is pretty well kept by the higher animals. They rarely kill their own kind: hawks do not prey upon hawks, nor foxes prey upon foxes, nor weasels upon weasels; but lower down this does not hold. Trout eat trout, and pickerel eat pickerel, and among the insects young spiders eat one another, and the female spider eats her mate, if she can get him. There is but little, if any, neighborly love among even the higher animals. They treat one another as rivals, or associate for mutual protection. One cow will lick and comb another in the most affectionate manner, and the next moment savagely gore her. Hate and cruelty for the most part rule in the animal world. A few of the higher animals are monogamous, but by far the greater number of species are polygamous or promiscuous. There is no mating or pairing in the great bovine tribe, and none among the rodents that I know of, or among the bear family, or the cat fam-

ily, or among the seals. When we come to the birds, we find mating, and occasional pairing for life, as with the ostrich and perhaps the eagle.

As for the rights of property among the animals, I do not see how we can know just how far those rights are respected among individuals of the same species. We know that bees will rob bees, and that ants will rob ants; but whether or not one chipmunk or one flying squirrel or one wood mouse will plunder the stores of another I do not know. Probably not, as the owner of such stores is usually on hand to protect them. Moreover, these provident little creatures all lay up stores in the autumn, before the season of scarcity

Julian Burroughs photographed his father bringing home the cows. The area around the Roxbury homestead was dairying country, and John Burroughs and his siblings were expert milkers. "My memory is fragrant with the breath of cattle," he wrote. "I come of a race of drivers of oxen, and milkers of cows."

sets in, and so have no need to plunder one another. In case the stores of one squirrel were destroyed by some means, and it were able to dispossess another of its hoard, would it not in that case be a survival of the fittest, and so conducive to the well-being of the race of squirrels?

I have never known any of our wild birds to steal the nesting-material of another bird of the same kind, but I have known birds to try to carry off the material belonging to other species.

But usually the rule of might is the rule of right among the animals. As to most of the other commandments,—of coveting, of bearing false witness, of honoring the father and the mother, and so forth,—how can these apply to the animals or have any biological value to them? Parental obedience among them is not a very definite thing. There is neither obedience nor disobedience, because there are no commands. The alarm-cries of the parents are quickly understood by the young, and their actions imitated in the presence of danger, all of which of course has a biological value.

The instances which Mr. Seton cites of animals fleeing to man for protection from their enemies prove to my mind only how the greater fear drives out the lesser. The hotly pursued animal sees a possible cover in a group of men and horses or in an unoccupied house, and rushes there to hide. What else could the act mean? So a hunted deer or sheep will leap from a precipice which, under ordinary circumstances, it would avoid. So would a man. Fear makes bold in such cases.

I certainly have found "good in everything,"—in all natural processes and products,—not the "good" of the Sunday-school books, but the good of natural law and order, the good of that system of things out of which we came and which is the source of our health and strength. It is good that fire should burn, even if it consumes your house; it is good that force should crush, even if it crushes you; it is good that rain should fall, even if it destroys your crops or floods your land. Plagues and pestilences attest the constancy of natural law. They set us to cleaning our streets and houses and to readjusting our relations to outward nature. Only in a live universe could disease and death prevail. Death is a phase of life, a redistributing of the type. Decay is another kind of growth.

Yes, good in everything, because law in everything, truth in everything, the sequence of cause and effect in everything, and it may all be good to me if on the right principles I relate my life to it. I can make the heat and the cold serve me, the winds and the floods, gravity and all the chemical and dynamical forces, serve me, if I take hold of them by the right handle. The bad in things arises from our abuse or misuse of them or from our wrong relations to them. A thing is good or bad according as it stands related to my constitution. We say the order of nature is rational; but is it not because our reason is the outcome of that order? Our well-being consists in learning it and in adjusting our lives to it. When we cross it or seek to contravene it, we are destroyed. But Nature in her universal procedures is not rational, as I am rational when I weed my garden, prune my trees, select my seed or my stock, or arm myself with tools or weapons. In such matters I take a short cut to that which Nature reaches by a slow, roundabout, and wasteful process. How does she weed her garden? By the survival of the fittest. How does she select her breeding-stock? By the law of battle; the strongest rules. Hers, I repeat, is a slow and wasteful process. She fertilizes the soil by plowing in the crop. She cannot take a short cut. She assorts and arranges her goods by the law of the winds and the tides. She builds up with one hand and pulls down with the other. Man changes the conditions to suit the things. Nature changes the things to suit the conditions. She adapts the plant or the animal to its environment. She does not drain her marshes; she fills them up. Hers is the larger reason—the reason of the All. Man's reason introduces a new method; it cuts across, modifies, or abridges the order of Nature.

I do not see design in Nature in the old teleological sense; but I see everything working to its own proper end, and that end is foretold in the means. Things are not designed; things are begotten. It is as if the final plan of a man's house, after he had begun to build it, should be determined by the winds and the rains and the shape of the ground upon which it stands. The eye is begotten by those vibrations in the ether called light, the ear by those vibrations in the air called sound, the sense of smell by those emanations called odors. There are probably other vibrations and emanations that we have no senses for because our well-being does not demand them.

We think it reasonable that a stone should fall and that smoke should rise because we have never known either of them to do the contrary. We think it reasonable that fire should burn and that frost should freeze, because this accords with universal experience. Thus, there is a large order of facts that are reasonable because they are invariable: the same effect always follows the same cause. Our reason is developed and disciplined by observing the order of Nature; and yet human rationality is of another order from the rationality of Nature. Man learns from Nature how to master and control her. He turns her currents into new channels; he spurs her in directions of his own. Nature has no economic or scientific rationality. She progresses by the method of trial and error. Her advance is symbolized by that of the child learning to walk. She experiments endlessly. Evolution has worked all around the horizon. In feeling her way to man she has produced thousands of other forms of life. The globe is peopled as it is because the creative energy was blind and did not at once find the single straight road to man. Had the law of variation worked only in one direction, man might have found himself the sole occupant of the universe. Behold the varieties of trees, of shrubs, of grasses, of birds, of insects, because Nature does not work as man does, with an eye single to one particular end. She scatters, she sows her seed upon the wind, she commits her germs to the waves and the floods. Nature is indifferent to waste, because what goes out of one pocket goes into another. She is indifferent to failure, because failure on one line means success on some other.

4

But I am not preaching much of a gospel, am I? Only the gospel of contentment, of appreciation, of heeding simple near-by things—a gospel the burden of which still is love, but love that goes hand in hand with understanding.

There is so much in Nature that is lovely and lovable, and so much that gives us pause. But here it is, and here we are, and we must make the most of it. If the ways of the Eternal as revealed in his works are past finding out, we must still unflinchingly face what our reason reveals to us. "Red in tooth and claw." Nature does not preach; she enforces, she executes. All her answers are yea, yea, or nay, nay. Of the virtues and beatitudes of which the gospel of Christ makes so much—meekness, forgiveness, self-denial, charity, love, holiness—she knows nothing. Put yourself in her way, and she crushes you; she burns you, freezes you, stings you, bites you, or devours you.

Yet I would not say that the study of Nature did not favor meekness or sobriety or gentleness or forgiveness or charity, because the great Nature students and prophets, like Darwin, would rise up and confound me. Certainly it favors seriousness, truthfulness, and simplicity of life; or, are only the serious and single-minded drawn to the study of Nature? I doubt very much if it favors devoutness or holiness, as those qualities are inculcated by the church, or any form of religious enthusiasm. Devoutness and holiness come of an attitude toward the universe that is in many ways incompatible with that implied by the pursuit of natural science. The joy of the Nature student like Darwin or any great naturalist is to know, to find out the reason of things and the meaning of things, to trace the footsteps of the creative energy; while the religious devotee is intent only upon losing himself in infinite being. True, there have been devout naturalists and men of science; but their devoutness did not date from their Nature studies, but from their training, or from the times in which they lived. Theology and science, it must be said, will not mingle much better than oil and water, and your devout scientist and devout Nature student lives in two separate compartments of his being at different times. Intercourse with Nature—I mean intellectual intercourse, not merely the emotional intercourse of the sailor or explorer or farmer—tends to beget a habit of mind the farthest possible removed from the myth-making, the vision-seeing, the voice-hearing habit and temper. In all matters relating to the visible,

In 1909 Burroughs was coaxed into making a trip to the Southwest. His old friend John Muir met him in Arizona and guided him through the Grand Canyon and other wonders of the region. Though of markedly different temperaments, the "two Johnnies" were lovers of solitude and literature.

concrete universe it substitutes broad daylight for twilight; it supplants fear with curiosity; it overthrows superstition with fact; it blights credulity with the frost of skepticism. I say frost of skepticism advisedly. Skepticism is a much more healthful and robust habit of mind than the limp, pale-blooded, non-resisting habit that we call credulity.

In intercourse with Nature you are dealing with things at first hand, and you get a rule, a standard, that serves you through life. You are dealing with primal sanities, primal honesties, primal attraction; you are touching at least the hem of the garment with which the infinite is clothed, and virtue goes out from it to you. It must be added that you are dealing with primal cruelty, primal blindness, primal wastefulness, also. Nature works with reference to no measure of time, no bounds of space, and no limits of material. Her economies are not our economies. She is prodigal, she is careless, she is indifferent; yet nothing is lost. What she lavishes with one hand, she gathers in with the other. She is blind, yet she hits the mark because she shoots in all directions. Her germs fill the air; the winds and the tides are her couriers. When you think you have defeated her, your triumph is hers; it is still by her laws that you reach your end.

We make ready our garden in a season, and plant our seeds and hoe our crops by some sort of system. Can any one tell how many hundreds of millions of years Nature has been making ready her garden and planting her seeds?

There can be little doubt, I think, but that intercourse with Nature and a knowledge of her ways tends to simplicity of life. We come more and more to see through the follies and vanities of the world and to appreciate the real values. We load ourselves up with so many false burdens, our complex civilization breeds in us so many false or artificial wants, that we become separated from the real sources of our strength and health as by a gulf.

For my part, as I grow older I am more and more inclined to reduce my baggage, to lop off superfluities. I become more and more in love with simple things and simple folk—a small house, a hut in the woods, a tent on the shore. The show and splendor of great houses, elaborate furnishings, stately halls, oppress me, impose upon me. They fix the attention upon false values, they set up a false standard of beauty; they stand between me and the real feeders of character and thought. A man needs a good roof over his head winter and summer, and a good chimney and a big wood-pile in winter. The more open his four walls are, the more fresh air he will get, and the longer he will live.

How the contemplation of Nature as a whole does take the conceit out of us! How we dwindle to mere specks and our little lives to the span of a moment in the presence of the cosmic bodies and the interstellar spaces! How we hurry! How we husband our time! A year, a month, a day, an hour may mean so much to us. Behold the infinite leisure of Nature!

A few trillions or quadrillions of years, what matters it to the Eternal? Jupiter and Saturn must be billions of years older than the earth. They are evidently yet passing through that condition of cloud and vapor and heat that the earth passed through untold aeons ago, and they will not reach the stage of life till aeons to come. But what matters it? Only man hurries. Only the Eternal has infinite time. When life comes to Jupiter, the earth will doubtless long have been a dead world. It may continue a dead world for aeons longer before it is melted up in the eternal crucible and recast, and set on its career of life again.

Familiarity with the ways of the Eternal as they are revealed in the physical universe certainly tends to keep a man sane and sober and safeguards him against the vagaries and half-truths which our creeds and indoor artificial lives tend to breed. Shut away from Nature, or only studying her through religious fears and superstitions, what a mess a large body of mankind in all ages have made of it! Think of the obsession of the speedy "end of the world" which has so often taken possession of whole communities, as if a world that has been an eternity in forming could end in a day, or on the striking of the clock! It is not many years since a college professor published a book figuring out, from some old historical documents and predictions, just the year in which the great mundane show would break up. When I was a small boy at school in the early forties, during the Millerite excitement about the approaching end of all mundane things, I remember, on the day when the momentous event was expected to take place, how the larger school-girls were thrown into a great state of alarm and agitation by a thundercloud that let down a curtain of rain, blotting out the mountain on the opposite side of the valley. "There it comes!" they said, and their tears flowed copiously. I remember that I did not share their fears, but watched the cloud, curious as to what the end of the world would be like. I cannot brag, as Thoreau did, when he said he would not go around the corner to see the world blow up. I am quite sure my curiosity would get the better of me and that I should go, even at this late day. Or think of the more harmless obsession of many good people about the second coming of Christ, or about the resurrection of the physical body when the last trumpet shall sound. A little natural knowledge ought to be fatal to all such notions. Natural knowledge shows us how transient and insignificant we are, and how vast and everlasting the world is, which was aeons before we were, and will be other aeons after we are gone, yea, after the whole race of man is gone. Natural knowledge takes the conceit out of us, and is the sure antidote to all our petty anthropomorphic views of the universe.

5

I was struck by this passage in one of the recently published letters of Saint-Gaudens: "The principal thought in my life is that we are on a planet going no one knows where, probably to something higher (on the Darwinian principle of evolution); that, whatever it is, the passage is terribly sad and tragic, and to bear up at times against what seems to be the Great Power that is over us, the practice of love, charity, and courage are the great things."

The "Great Power" that is over us does seem unmindful of us as individuals, if it does not seem positively against us, as Saint-Gaudens seemed to think it was.

Surely the ways of the Eternal are not as our ways. Our standards of prudence, of economy, of usefulness, of waste, of delay, of failure — how far off they seem from the scale upon which the universe is managed or deports itself! If the earth should be blown to pieces to-day, and all life instantly blotted out, would it not be just like what we know of the cosmic prodigality and indifference? Such appalling disregard of all human motives and ends bewilders us.

Of all the planets of our system probably only two or three are in a condition to sustain life. Mercury, the youngest of them all, is doubtless a dead world, with absolute zero on one side and a furnace temperature on the other. But what matters it? Whose loss or gain is it? Life seems only an incident in the universe, evidently not an end. It appears or it does not appear, and who shall say yea or nay? The asteroids at one time no doubt formed a planet between Mars and Jupiter. Some force which no adjective can describe or qualify blew it into fragments, and there, in its stead, is this swarm of huge rocks making their useless rounds in the light of the sun forever and ever. What matters it to the prodigal All? Bodies larger than our sun collide in the depths of space before our eyes with results so terrific that words cannot even hint them. The last of these collisions—of this "wreck of matter and crush of worlds"—reported itself to our planet in February, 1901, when a star of the twelfth magnitude suddenly blazed out as a star of the first magnitude and then slowly faded. It was the grand finale of the independent existence of two enormous celestial bodies. They apparently ended in dust that whirled away in the vast abyss of siderial space, blown by the winds upon which suns and systems drift as autumn leaves. It would be quite in keeping with the observed ways of the Eternal, if these bodies had had worlds in their train, teeming with life, which met the same fate as the central colliding bodies.

Does not force as we know it in this world go its own way with the same disregard of the precious thing we call life? Such long and patient preparations for it,—apparently the whole stellar system in labor pains to bring it forth,— and yet held so cheaply and indifferently in the end! The small insect that just now alighted in front of my jack-plane as I was dressing a timber, and was reduced to a faint yellow stain upon the wood, is typical of the fate of man before the unregarding and unswerving terrestrial and celestial forces. The great wheels go round just the same whether they are crushing the man or crushing the corn for his bread. It is all one to the Eternal. Flood, fire, wind, gravity, are for us or against us indifferently. And yet the earth is here, garlanded with the seasons and riding in the celestial currents like a ship in calm summer seas, and man is here with all things under his feet. All is well in our corner of the universe. The great mill has made meal of our grist and not of the miller. We have taken our chances and have won. More has been for us than against us. During the little segment of time that man has been upon the earth, only one great calamity that might be called cosmical has befallen it. The ice age of one or two hundred thousand years was

such a calamity. But man survived it. The spring came again, and life, the traveler, picked itself up and made a new start. But if he had not survived it, if nothing had survived it, the great procession would have gone on just the same; the gods would have been just as well pleased.

The battle is to the strong, the race is to the fleet. This is the order of nature. No matter for the rest, for the weak, the slow, the unlucky, so that the fight is won, so that the race of man continues. You and I may fail and fall before our time; the end may be a tragedy or a comedy. What matters it? Only some one must succeed, will succeed.

We are here, I say, because, in the conflict of forces, the influences that made for life have been in the ascendant. This conflict of forces has been a part of the process of our development. We have been ground out as between an upper and a nether millstone, but we have squeezed through, we have actually arrived, and are all the better for the grinding—all those who have survived. But, alas for those whose lives went out in the crush! Maybe they often broke the force of the blow for us.

Nature is not benevolent; Nature is just, gives pound for pound, measure for measure, makes no exceptions, never tempers her decrees with mercy, or winks at any infringement of her laws. And in the end is not this best? Could the universe be run as a charity or a benevolent institution, or as a poor-house of the most approved pattern? Without this merciless justice, this irrefragable law, where should we have brought up long ago? It is a hard gospel; but rocks are hard too, yet they form the foundations of the hills.

Man introduces benevolence, mercy, altruism, into the world, and he pays the price in his added burdens; and he reaps his reward in the vast social and civic organizations that were impossible without these things.

I have no doubt that the life of man upon this planet will end, as all other forms of life will end. But the potential man will continue and does continue on other spheres. One cannot think of one part of the universe as producing man, and no other part as capable of it. The universe is all of a piece so far as its material constituents are concerned; that we know. Can there be any doubt that it is all of a piece so far as its invisible and intangible forces and capabilities are concerned? Can we believe that the earth is an alien and a stranger in the universe? that it has no near kin? that there is no tie of blood, so to speak, between it and the other planets and systems? Are the planets not all of one family, sitting around the same central source of warmth and life? And is not our system a member of a still larger family or tribe, and it of a still larger, all bound together by ties of consanguinity? Size is nothing, space is nothing. The worlds are only red corpuscles in the arteries.

of the infinite. If man has not yet appeared on the other planets, he will in time appear, and when he has disappeared from this globe, he will still continue elsewhere.

I do not say that he is the end and aim of creation; it would be logical, I think, to expect a still higher form. Man has been man but a little while comparatively, less than one hour of the twenty-four of the vast geologic day; a few hours more and he will be gone; less than another geologic day like the past, and no doubt all life from the earth will be gone. What then? The game will be played over and over again in other worlds, without approaching any nearer the final end than we are now. There is no final end, as there was no absolute beginning, and can be none with the infinite.

Time and Change

When his brother Eden died in 1919, John Burroughs was the sole survivor of his family. Saddened by the loss of so many friends and relatives, he wrote, "One of the drawbacks of old age is that one outlives his generation and feels alone in the world. The new generations have interests of their own, and are no more in sympathy with you than you are with them. The octogenarian has no alternative but to live in the past. He lives with the dead, and they pull him down."

To individualize is the secret of observation. In one sense the great poet, and the great naturalist, are the same—things take definite and distinct shape to them; they are capable of vivid impressions. The naturalist walks the real world with his eyes open; he knows a man from a stump at once. The poet walks the ideal world, and his eye disintegrates in the same way.

The Heart of Burroughs's Journals

Unadulterated, unsweetened observations are what the real nature-lover craves. No man can invent incidents and traits as interesting as the reality. Then, to know that a thing is true gives it such a savor! The truth—how we do crave the truth! We cannot feed our minds on simulacra any more than we can our bodies. Do assure us that the thing you tell is true. If you must counterfeit the truth, do it so deftly that we shall never detect you. But in natural history there is no need to counterfeit the truth; the reality always suffices, if you have eyes to see it and ears to hear it.

Ways of Nature

Our northern November day itself is like spring water. It is melted frost, dissolved snow. There is a chill in it and an exhilaration also. The forenoon is all morning and the afternoon all evening. The shadows seem to come forth and to revenge themselves upon the day. The sunlight is diluted with darkness. The colors fade from the landscape, and only the sheen of the river lights up the gray and brown distance.

Winter Sunshine

If the October days were a cordial like the sub-acids of fruits, these are a tonic like the wine of iron. Drink deep, or be careful how you taste this December vintage. The first sip may chill, but a full draught warms and invigorates.

Winter Sunshine

The country is more of a wilderness, more of a wild solitude, in the winter than in the summer. The wild comes out. The urban, the cultivated, is hidden or negatived. You hardly know a good field from a poor, a meadow from a pasture, a park from a forest. Lines and boundaries are disregarded; gates and bar-ways are unclosed; man lets go his hold upon the earth; title-deeds are deep buried beneath the snow; the best-kept grounds relapse to a state of nature; under the pressure of the cold, all the wild creatures become outlaws, and roam abroad beyond their usual haunts . . . . In fact, winter, like some great calamity, changes the status of most creatures and sets them adrift. Winter, like poverty, makes us acquainted with strange bedfellows.

Signs and Seasons

The simplicity of winter has a deep moral. The return of nature, after such a career of splendor and prodigality, to habits so simple and austere, is not lost upon either the head or the heart. It is the philosopher coming back from the banquet and the wine to a cup of water and a crust of bread.

Winter Sunshine

...one has no privacy with Nature now, and does not wish to seek her in nooks and hidden ways. She is not at home if he goes there; her house is shut up and her hearth cold...

Winter Sunshine
